Acknowledgements

Four of the stories in this collection are reprinted from the *New Statesman*, whose permission to make use of them here is gratefully acknowledged.

CONTENTS

OUT with the Girls   9

UP the Junction   15

THE Gold Blouse   23

THE Deserted House   31

DINNER Hour   39

SUNDAY Morning   45

WEDDING Anniversary   51

THE Clipjoint   59

BANG on the Common   69

WASH Night   79

OUT with the Boys   87

THE Trial   93

PRISON Visit   99

DEATH of an Old Scrubber   105

THE Tally Man   111

THE Children   125

<u>OUT</u> with the girls

We stand, the three of us, me, Sylvie and Rube, pressed up against the saloon door, brown ales clutched in our hands. Rube, neck stiff so as not to shake her beehive, stares sultrily round the packed pub. Sylvie eyes the boy hunched over the mike and shifts her gaze down to her breasts snug in her new pink jumper. 'Kiss! Kiss! Kiss!' he screams. Three blokes beckon us over to their table.

'Fancy 'em?'

Rube doubles up with laughter. 'Come on, then. They can buy us some beer.'

'Hey, look out, yer steppin' on me winkle!'

Dignified, the three of us squeeze between tables and sit ourselves, knees tight together, daintily on the chairs.

'Three browns, please,' says Sylvie before we've been asked.

'I've seen you in here before, ain't I?' A boy leans luxuriously against the leather jacket slung over the back of his chair.

'Might 'ave done.'

'You come from Battersea, don't yer?'

'Yeah, me and Sylvie do. She don't though. She's an heiress from Chelsea.'

'Really? You really an heiress?' Jimmy Dean moves his chair closer to mine, sliding his arm along the back.

'Are yer married?'

'Course she is. What do yer think that is? Scotch mist?' Rube points to my wedding ring.

Sylvie says, 'Bet they're all married, dirty ginks!'

'Like to dance?'

Rube moves onto the floor. She hunches up her shoulders round her ears, sticks out her lower lip and swings in time to the shattering music.

'What's it like havin' a ton of money?'

'You can't buy love.'

'No, but you can buy a bit of the other.' Sylvie chokes, spewing out brown ale.

'I'd get a milk-white electric guitar.'

'Yeah and a milk-white Cadillac convertible—walk in the shop and peel off the notes. Bang 'em down on the counter and drive out—that's what yer dad does, I bet . . .'

We were crushed in the toilets. All round girls smeared on pan-stick.

'I can't go with him, he's too short.'

'All the grey glitter I put on me hair come off on his cheek and I hadn't the heart to tell him.'

'I wouldn't mind goin' with a married man 'cept I couldn't abear him goin' home and gettin' into bed with his wife.'

'Me hair all right?'

'Yeah, lend us yer lacquer.'

'Now don't get pissin' off and leavin' me.' Rube pulled at her mauve skirt so it clung to her haunches and stopped short of her round knees.

Outside revving bikes were splitting the night.

'Where we going?'

'Let's go swimmin' up the Common.'

'We ain't got no swim-suits with us.'

'We'll swim down one end and you down the other. It's dark, ain't it?'

'Who do yer think's going to see yer? The man in the moon?'

'Yeah and what's to stop yer hands wandering?'

'We'll tie 'em behind our backs.'

'Here, I'll never git on there I can't get me knees apart.'

'Hitch yer skirt up under yer coat.'

'Help, me grandmother'll catch cold!'

The three of us climb onto the bikes, each behind a boy. We burn up Tooting Broadway and streak round a corner.

'I did this bend at eighty once,' he shouts over my shoulder.

'Ninety-two people bin decapitated on them iron girders, taking it too fast.' We race across the common, then shudder to a halt under some trees. He wears jeans, black boots with double gold buckles and a fine lawn shirt beneath his un-zipped jacket.

'There are two things I'd like to be—a racing driver or a pilot. But you've gotta have money for that.'

We clambered over the high wall, pulled and pushed by the boys, went giggling through the coke pile to where the gleaming pool lay. Huddled beneath the cabin eaves, we watched the naked boys plunge into the thick water.

'I wouldn't trust Ronnie, you can tell by his eyes.'

'I'm bloody well going to keep me drawers on.'

A train howls by across the Common, a flickering light in the crowded trees, and then darkness except for an orange glow from distant street lamps.

I swim off towards the dark end. He puts an arm around my neck and I see tattooed on his greenish-white skin I AM ELVIS. Suddenly we are lit up. Search-lights. The law.

'Quick, me clobber!' Rube is running towards me, bulging out of her bra, a pink jelly, her black hair wet down her back. Jimmy grabs my wrist and we run into the trees. He rubs his blond hair dry on his shirt.

'Sometimes we go camping. Take tents and something to cover you over and go down to the seaside. The girls tell their mums they're going camping four or five together and then they come with us—fabulous sleeping out with a bird to keep yer warm.

'All I want is a bike and ten pounds a week in me pocket —there's one thing I can't stand and that's being skint.

'Comin' home with me? There's a place I know, matter of fact it's right in the buildings. I'm the only one what knows it. I nick me mum's key to the wash-house, she's got an old mattress tied up in there—I just untie it.'

Sylvie's laugh rips the night. 'Hey, you two, we're going!'

'I bet she's well away!'

'Know what happened in work today? I was sittin' on the steps outside McCrindle's eatin' me dinner when this Fred, Indian gink, says, "Look out, love, I can see yer drawers." So I says, "What colour are they then??" "Pink," he says. "No, they're not," I says, "because I ain't got none on." '

'You work up McCrindle's?'

'Yeah, I've had a scrub, so don't go saying you can smell the butter on me.'

Sylvie whispers, 'He undid me brassieres, so I told him to do them up again. "You certainly know where the hook is," I says.'

' 'E believes in grabbin' hold of yer and bitin' yer ear-'ole.'

'I like it rough. You get more feelin' out of it that way.'

'I was tuckin' in his shirt for him and he says, "Don't put yer hand down there or you'll get a shock!" '

The boys pushed the bikes out of the trees and once again we shot off into the night.

'I've never bin beaten except once in a burn-up on the Sidcup mile. Then I found the other bloke dead at the end. He hit an island—peaceful he looked, no blood nor nothing.' We were standing in the concrete stairwell of some LCC flats.

A ball of paper blew about. A girl in stilettos clattered down the stairs. 'Cor, we used to belt along that road, round the bends, and the girls would be lollin' on the banks wavin' and callin' out, "Give us a ride . . ." '

'Yeah, let's face it, it's dicin' with death, it's gettin' just that inch in front . . .'

'You must think I'm slow. I don't know what to say to a decent girl. If you was an old slag, I'd just say, "Come 'ere . . ." '

'All me mates are gettin' married, it's the rage . . .'

'I went steady once, but she broke it off after me accident. I remember openin' me eyes and seein' me mate carryin' me shoe across the road. "That's it," I thought, "I've lost me bloody foot!" And I passed out for twenty-four hours. When I come to, it was still there . . .'

'Yeah, when me mates get to twenty or twenty-one, they see the girls they mucked around with getting married and they think, "if I don't hurry up all the best ones will be gone." So they get married and then they're bloody miserable . . .'

'Is it ever wrong to do what you want to?'

He leant back against the concrete wall, scrawled over with chalk drawings and girl's names, the silver chain taut against his narrow throat. Then he says. 'Do me a favour.'

'What is it?'

'Seduce me.'

UP the junction

It is Saturday afternoon. I go over to knock for Rube. A small man with a pork-pie hat and a black book is standing outside the door.

'No one in?' I ask. He shrugs his shoulders, so I open the letter-box and holler, 'Rube!' Mysteriously the door opens and I walk into the kitchen where they are: Sylvie ironing a shirt, Bert writing betting slips.

'Rube's still in bed. You can go up, and tell him to piss off —it's only the Tally Man—Mum owes him for four pair of sheets.'

So, 'Mrs Macarthy isn't in,' I tell him. But he puts his foot inside the door and says in a guttural voice, 'Tell her I want ter see her.' There is a creaking on the stairs and I see Mrs Macarthy creeping down and pressing herself against the wall as she makes for the kitchen.

'I can hear you, Mrs Macarthy!' he shouts. With a mixed expression of humour and fury she shouts back, 'Go and get it off of Mrs O'Sullivan, go and knock her door down.'

'No need for that, she's paying very well,' he shouts back.

'I'll give him a couple of bob.' Sylvie picks up her purse and takes out a two-bob piece. 'That's got rid of him,' she says, coming back. 'He says Mrs O'Sullivan really is paying all right.'

Upstairs Rube has thrown off all her covers. She lies on the bed in her baby doll pyjamas surrounded by black hair. Her white face is cross as she opens her sleep-heavy eyes; then she smiles, stretching bare white legs and looking round the room at the pile of worn blankets and the underclothes strewn across the lino patterned floor and the pink plastic curlers on the mantelpiece. While she dresses I look out the window over the lavatory and the six brown hens picking in the dust and the two white rabbits.

"Come on then.'

We go downstairs. 'Anyone want anything up the Junction?'

Rube stands on tiptoe to put on her Mediterranean Tan pan-stick in the kitchen mirror.

'Yeah, get me some stockings—three-and-eleven bare-leg.'

The builders from the new flats whistle as we go past the corner shop—nylon film panties one-and-three pegged between the tinned peas and plastic toys—arm in arm with the sun jumping off the pavement.

'I met this fella up the park, he lifted me right off the ground. His name's Terry, he's got a Triumph six-fifty. He said he was lookin' for a wife . . . I says he'd have to get rid of that motorbike afore I went steady with him. He laughs and says, "We'll see about that!" I'm almost frightened to go with him because I know he'll be able to do anything he wants with me . . . I'm meetin' him tomorrer, seven-thirty. He told me to wear a pair of jeans . . .'

'Let's knock at Ada's.'

Ada opens the door crying: her little brother had burnt all her clothes. 'He set fire to the pram where I keeps them . . .' We go into the kitchen where her mother sits quite still on a chair only one week out of Banstead. There is water and dirt all over the floor. Ada shouts at her mother to help her clear it up. She doesn't answer. In Ada's room the floor is covered with clean newspaper. In one corner are two arm-chairs pushed together with some blankets folded neatly on top. 'It's me birthday tomorrer . . .' Her green winkle-pickers stand neatly against the wall and in the middle of it all stands the smouldering pram. Out in the front passage ten pigeons fly about. 'Aren't they beauties? Aren't they darlings?' says her dad. 'I have to keep the windows sealed in case one escapes.'

'Cheerio, Ada.' We hurry out into the street.

'Cor,' says Rube, 'what a stink.'

'Hello, Mrs Hardy.'

'Hello, ducks. I'm just looking for me hat—it blew off me head yesterday in the wind and I couldn't find it! I lost another sister yesterday. That's two this month—me brother at the beginning and me sister at the end—it's bin a bad year. I lost me other brother January, but I keep smilin'. I've still got a brother and a sister left . . .'

Past some torn-down prefabs and we walk over the erupted

foundations looking for the drains. 'There's a gorgeous bloke what works in the breadshop. Shall we go in?' In we go and buy two fourpenny pies and out again. 'Oh shame, he weren't in there.'

'Coming dancing tonight up the North Pole?'

'See that fellow? June went with him. He made her get in the back of his ten-ton truck and wouldn't let her out till she give in.'

'See him? Patsy Chubb had it with him twice in his car

and his wife's carrying. Sylvie was thinking of going up and telling her.'

'Oh, she shouldn't do that.'

'Why not? She's got a right to know.'

'It'll only upset her. What's the point?'

'You're different from us; it doesn't matter if your old man does piss off with someone else, but she'd have to go on the National Assistance and starve.'

'See her: she done her house up all posh and filled it with Coloureds—tasty like the black and white minstrel show. "What you after, a bit of jungle juice?" Sylvie asked her.'

We turn a corner past a giant bulldozer crashing through the slums. In the mud lies a split suitcase with a rag mat tied about by the *Daily Mirror*. Under the tunnel trains whistle and thunder above us and out into the Arcade. Four or five girls stand outside the shoe-shop admiring the latest creations: 'Handmade shoes £3 a pair.'

'See them red boots. June's got them. I'm not speaking to her no more. We had a row last night over your place when we was baby-sitting. These two blokes come down for us and she wanted the bed. "You can have the sofa; I'm having the bed and we'll change half way if you like." But she made a big fuss. Me lips aren't half sore. You get a funny taste in your mouth after you've been snoggin', don't yer?'

We go into the chemist. 'I want a black rinse, please, with blue lights in it. I was going to bleach it, but then Sylvie said I'd look like a Belisha beacon on a dark night.'

'I think I'll weigh myself.' I take off my coat and shoes.

'Fatty, you're nine stone three. Better take yer jumper off as well!' The chemist stands by watching. 'Are you working, Ruby? I need a girl to serve on cosmetics.'

'I'm working down McCrindle's, thank you, Mr Cream.'

We go on past the coffee shop with the boys leaning outside. 'Hey, look, she's melted my ice!'

'When I was fifteen that new type of kissin' come in where they stick their tongue right into yer mouth—this bloke done it to me and he had such a long tongue he half choked me.'

'Britain's answer to the H-bomb!' Rube turns up her nose and sticks out her chest as she prances by. 'They reckon he was choppin' it off with his last assistant.'

We go past the furniture shop. 'Why don't you get yourself a decent bedroom suite? I've known plenty of poor people—we've been poor ourselves—but I've never heard of no one sleeping on a mattress propped up on books. Sylvie got a suite £108 when she married Ted. She's going to give that one to me and put down on a new one when she goes to live with Ray. She won't choose it till they get a place, though; otherwise, it'll look old-fashioned before they get it out the shop.'

'Shall we go up the Pay-as-You-Wear shop and choose a couple of frocks?'

'I though you were skint.'

'Pay as you wear, berk! You only have to put down about fifteen bob deposit.'

'And then you pay the rest off weekly?'

'Yer meant to but you don't bother. Sylvie got a fabulous

two-piece up there; one pound down and she wasn't going to pay no more. When they sent her this letter she rings up and says, "I'm Miss Macarthy's mother. I'm afraid they've taken her away to Banstead Mental Home." But they sent her a red note saying they was putting the matter to the solicitors, so she's rung up again and said, "It's so sad, Miss Macarthy's passed away, so please don't send no more letters." '

'Let's go in Scala's for a cup of tea.'

We sit down at a table. 'Hello, Pauline,' says Rube.

Pauline wears a white silk head-scarf around her tiny face marked with a painted beauty spot. She says, 'I'm going out to Jersey for four months this season. Five pound a week and all yer keep. I met a gorgeous fellow out there last year. He was really big-built' (she gestures across her scanty bosom) 'muscular, lovely looking fella—blond hair. He knows I'm coming this year.' She is pretty in the dirty café; full ashtrays and dripping sauce bottles; sugar-bowls with brown clotted lumps in the white sugar. 'I've broken off me engagement but I've kept the ring.'

She dives her hand into her bag and takes out a little white cardboard box with a tiny diamond ring embedded in velveteen. 'I was so depressed at first I started going to evenin' classes.'

'Any good fellas there?' asked Rube, drumming her heels on the floor.

'No—I only went twice, then I give it up.'

'It's silly to go to evenin' classes. After all you're only young once—you can spend all yer time at evenin' classes when yer an old bag.'

A record drops and a high painful boy's voice sings:

> *Oh come on, take me by the hand*
> *And lead me to the land*
>   *Of Ecstasy—Oh Ecstasy!*

THE gold blouse

'ANYONE LEND me their husband for the week-end?'

'Yeah, you can 'ave mine, he's a dirty sod on the quiet.'

'I'd lend you mine, only he wouldn't be much good to yer!'

'Send them all up. You know where I live—just by the church.'

'Do you like 'em fair or dark?'

'It's not their 'air I'm interested in!'

We laugh, twenty-five women hunched over three long tables, packing cheap sweets for Christmas. Thick red fingers, swollen with the cold, flash from tray to box. In a matter of seconds it's neatly packed, a little circle of sweets with three pink mice in the middle.

The factory only has two rooms; the one I am in is where we wrap and pack, twisting the bright paper around each sweet, licking labels and sticking them on top—*Cognac, Cointreau, Dolcis et Forte*—pretend liqueurs tasting of sickly sweet cordials. And the other one where the sweets are made; and a rickety conveyor belt moves the coloured centres under dripping chocolate.

'I started me diet today,' hunch-back Sheila shouts to me, her voice mingling with the music pouring out from high on the damp wall: 'I remember you, you're the one who made my dreams come true . . . Yes I do . . .' Dirt hangs in loops around the loudspeaker, '. . . When my life is through, and the angels ask me to recall the thrill of them all . . .' Sheila moves her head in eight-bar time. Her neck is thickly swaddled in a dirty yellow scarf and her hair sticks out stiff over the collar of her coat.

'Are you allowed to eat any?'

'You are if you don't get caught.'

Behind me Lily and Rube, the sorters slinging the sweets skilfully into the boxes, twist and talk alternately.

'She don't really care. I'd do meself in!'

'So would I. Do me nutter in.'

'Let's hope the baby don't inherit her hunch.'

'It's one thing when it's the bloke you're going to marry, but when you don't even know who it is . . .'

'Perhaps he done it in the dark.'

'I wouldn't be surprised—she's that daft!'

On my other side an old woman spits into a rag and wipes her hands over—'Got the guitar, get it every winter. Used to be a laundry you know—that's why it's so damp. Can't heat it, it would melt the chocolates. I nearly married a soldier. I was going with him two years, but then he showed me this letter from a girl in the ATS, said it was just playing about. But if they do it before marriage they do it after so I said I was through with him. He cried like a baby. I saw him once in Woolworth's when I was carrying me last child and I had such a lump in me throat I couldn't say nothing. I had to run out. My name would be Mrs Stacey now instead of Mrs Smith.'

My eyes began to ache in the cold electric light. There are no windows in the room where we have been sitting since eight in the morning earning our two-and-fivepence an hour —tenpence an hour for the under eighteens. The siren hoots. 'Tea's up. Go and get some sugar, Bent Sheil!'

'I'll come with you.' Bent Sheila and I go up the broken staircase to the loft and turn on the light. Mice scuttle. She dips the chipped mug into an open sack.

'Got any brothers and sisters, Sheila?'

'No, there's just me and me mum. You might think I was spoilt, being the only one, but I'm not really, you know.'

'Do you ever go danciny, Sheila?'

'No, but I go up the caff. The boys take me upstairs where it's dark.'

I thrust my cup under the urn and watch it fill with grey tea, then follow Rube and Lily into the cloakroom. There are no chairs. We sit on the concrete floor among bicycles, leaning our heads against the coats that hang from the walls.

Joyce, a girl with long auburn hair caught back with two pink slides, cuddles in a corner eating some cold chips out of a bit of newspaper.

'When are you getting married, Joyce?'

'Next month, when I'm sixteen.'

'Bit young, ain't yer?'

'No use waiting till yer an old crab is there?'

'Have you got yer trousseau ready yet?'

'No.'

'Are yer going to wear yer pink pyjamas?'

'No, me birthday suit.'

'Hear that? Joyce's going to have a naked ball.'

'Don't be filthy.'

'It's nice filth though.'

'Never mind Joyce, it's smashing!' said old Mrs Gordon, her arthritic fingers sticking stiffly out from black mitts.

Over the lavatories next door hangs a notice. WASH YOUR HANDS AFTER USING THE TOILETS. THIS IS A FOOD FACTORY. I call Rube. 'Could you come over here a minute please?'

'Listen to that. We've got to take her in hand—teach her how to speak. You say, "Rube, fuck you, get over here, mate!" '

'Know where I can find a towel?'

'There ain't one. Don't wash yer hands love, it'll take them five minutes to thaw out. Anyways, what the eye don't see the heart don't grieve.'

'Give us a hand with the urn.'

Two of the girls empty the tea-urn down the lavatory. 'Look at this! A packet of Weights at the bottom.'

THE gold blouse

'I thought it tasted sour.'

Lily is fooling with a bicycle.

'Wait for me, love.' Rube climbs on in front of Lily, holds her round the waist and pokes her with the point of the

saddle. Sheila giggles. 'Like a sandwich?' I take one and bite into the thick bread smeared with lemon curd.

'Me dad sleeps downstairs and I sleep upstairs with me mum. Me mum hasn't slept with me dad for ten years— she's had seven children and the doctor says it would kill her to have any more. Anyways she doesn't want to sleep with me dad now—he's a bad-tempered old sod.'

'Here they have a lot of fun . . . twistin' the night away . . .' the music swings out.

'Come on, Rube!' Lily throws the bike against the wall. Rube draws in her stomach, making the CANDY embroidered on her pocket stand out.

'See the man in evening clothes . . . How he got hit right on the nose . . .' Lily bends back and Rube, shaking her violent shoulders, leans over her, thrusting a slinky leg between her twisting thighs.

'Come on, Sheil, let's see you!'

Grinning, Sheila clambers to her feet and sways her heavy body to the beat, clutching her coat at the stomach. 'Oh man, there ain't nothing like . . . Twistin' the night away.'

'Well done, Sheila!' The women crowd around, shouting encouragement. 'Learn it in the ATS, Sheil?'

Excited by the sudden rush of attention, she sticks out her stiff hands and waves her plump leg, purplish from the cold.

'Take yer overcoat off, Sheil, and let yerself go!' Rube and Lily stop dancing and join the onlookers. The room is thick with the smell of fresh sweat. The music blares on . . . 'See the fella in blue jeans, dancing with the older queen, who's dolled up in a diamond ring . . . Twistin', twistin', twistin' the night away.'

Sheila opens her mouth, swaying desperately. As the music reaches its climax she flings off her coat revealing a gold damask blouse. 'Oh man, you oughta see him go . . .

Twistin', twistin', twistin' the night away.' It's over and she stands still in the hot circle of women, a laconic grin wide over her face, her richly embroidered Victorian blouse pushed into her old tweed skirt.

'Hey, look at that!'

'Wow, what a blouse!'

'Where did you get that Sheil, off the barrows?'

'Life's so drab you've got to wear something bright, ain't you, Sheil?'

'Me mum bought it for me.' Her scrawny arms stick out from the delicately puffed sleeves.

'Don't fib—one of yer boy-friends up the café gave it you.'

'Go and join the ATS in that!'

'Pity they've cleaned up the streets.'

Sheila giggled with coy pleasure, thrusting her chin down into the yellow scarf still wound about her neck.

"Tell you what, Sheila, we'll cut the sleeves off for you, that'll look better!'

With a giant pair of scissors amidst a great deal of cat calls, Rube did it.

'There you are, love, all set for the Jazz Band Ball.'

The blouse had large arm-holes, and now Sheila's grubby bra was exposed.

'I can see the scruff under your arms, Sheil!' There were howls of laughter.

'Here, Lily, let's give her a low back.' Rube grabbed the scissors and cut a V. The blouse slid sideways revealing a torn vest. The door opened. 'Back to work you women.'

Sheila, still grinning, sat down hugging her arms to her chest till someone threw her a worn cardigan. On the brown lino, amid discarded sweet papers and cigarette ends, the gold sleeves lay gleaming in the raw electric light.

THE deserted house

WE ARE at a party in a block of LCC flats: plates of ham sandwiches, crates of brown ale and Babycham, the radio-gram in the lounge, pop-song oblivion with the volume knob turned to full:

> *I go out of my mind*
> *When you're out of my arms . . .*

Rube, face deadpan, dances the Madison, brown velvet skirt, red patent sling-backs.

The record finishes. She whispers in my ear, 'Isn't he a darlin'? I don't half fancy a snog tonight.' Her black hair hangs long and thick. 'He's a couchty-mouch. After going steady for six months you get a bit fed up, snoggin' with the same bloke every night. And I've noticed when we're out Terry'll start staring at some other bird. He'll say to me, "You all right, love?" And then his eyes will wander off and get affixiated on some silly cow. "What are you lookin' at then?" I says. "Am I so borin'?" '

The thick-set fellow comes over and holds out a hand to Rube. 'You Romeo,' she says, following him onto the floor, a faint smell of hair-oil and a brown suit.

Out on the concrete balcony dusky Fulham stretches away.

'My wife went for me this morning when I was lying in bed, hit me on the back of the neck,' says Dave. The lights of Stamford Bridge Saturday-night football. Little rows of houses cluster round the gasworks. 'I should never have got married. Im not the marrying sort.'

> *My heart breaks up inside*
> *With the tears that I cry*
> *And I'm out of my mind over you.*

Sylvie comes over with a bloke. 'This is me mate I was telling you about.'

The boys talk. 'I was working on this posh flat up in Hampstead. We'd just finished the bathroom, all pink tiles, and I fancied a bath. So I goes in and I'm havin' a lovely soak when the lady whose place it is comes in to have a look around and the boys, instead of telling her I'm havin' a toilet or something lets her walk right into the bathroom and she sees me in the nude and gives a great scream . . .'

'Surprised she didn't jump on yer . . .'

'You girls like to come over the One-O-One?'

Out in the road the six of us pile into the beat-up Buick.
Rube and I sit up the back on the rolled-down hood.

'You don't drive a big flash car—you—on your money
we can't go far.'

'Shut yer mouth, Rube, you'll get a sore throat!'

'Well, I've got to open something and I can't open me
legs.'

The car slews to a stop. Dave lifts me off the back. We go
through a bricklayers' yard and down some filthy stone steps.
The club is an old cellar poshed up with hardboard and
flashy paper. 'Got two thousand pound' worth of gear in
'ere. There's that one-armed bandit—a hundred and fifty
nicker. They pin-tables, you can win fifteen pound on
them—they cost a thousand. And that new American-style
juke-box, that cost over a thousand.'

Outside in the yard the toilet is aswim with piss. Rube
blacks her eyebrows. 'Terry doesn't reckon I should go out
with anyone but him, but I tell him straight, "I ain't got
no rings on my fingers 'cept me own!"'

'Has Dave kissed yer tonight? You wanta get him worked
up. Give him a love-bite, that'll get him at it."

'Tom and Ronnie are going to do a clothes factory and
get us each a new rig-out.'

'Sylvie was well away in the back row at the New
Vic. They put us right up the front so we couldn't do
nothin'. I was choked.'

Back in the club the music blares out of the juke-box.
Rube dances, hands up and down thighs.

'I haven't half studied the form on that bird.'

'I reckon I'm the only one out of this lot what's at work.'

'You bin swimmin', Sylv?'

'Yeah.'

'I wondered why you looked so clean.'

She cuffs him in the stomach and he catches her hands. 'Come and dance.'

The constant ring of the bells on the pin-table, the flashing lights and numbers. Dave leans back against the wall. 'I got three years Borstal for me first offence. I reckon the judge didn't like the look of me. "How much lead you took?" he says to me. "One and a half ton," I says, "ripped off all the roofs in the fairground." '

Rube and her Romeo join us. 'Who's comin' bowlin'?"

'Ent got no money.'

'I've got plenty of money.' He unbuttons his pocket and shows the top of a ten-shilling note.

'Half a bleedin' quid—that's not money!'

'Comin' down to Southend this week-end? We take a crate of beer and have a right piss-up on the beach . . .'

'Me mate Johnny fell thirty feet off the scaffolding Friday. He's still unconscious. The foreman's trying to rig it, says he had a hole in his shoe and it tripped him over backwards, but really there weren't no safety rails . . .'

'Bin up the Lyceum lately, Tom?'

'I go up there Monday nights for a giggle—Continental dancing—but you offer to take a bird home and most of them live right out in the suburbs, so you find yerself walkin' home twenty miles if you haven't got a bike . . .'

'Let's go. It's dead in here.'

Outside the night is soft. We pile into the Buick and

cruise through the park. A smell of damp flowers and black trees against the mauve sky and the coloured beads of light trimming its neck.

Then among the houses the car stops. 'What's up?' 'We're going for a walk.' Tom and Kath get out of the car and march off into the night. Romeo twists Rube's body round towards him.

'Let's get out,' says Dave. 'I can't take you home because me mum's pawned all the furniture.' It is about three in the morning. The sky is navy-blue. We walk across a chaos of grass and rubble to a row of deserted houses. 'This is where we lived till it got demolished—slum clearance. They moved us out to lousy Roehampton.' He strikes a match and looks through a broken window. 'Comin' in?'

Strewn over the torn-up wooden boards lie—a bicycle wheel, two mattresses and a pair of National Health glasses. We go upstair. There are just two rooms, one off each side. 'When I saw yer sittin' there I began to sizzle: "I'm in it tonight," I thought. Then you began to talk and I realised you were a nice girl. I used to be a hospital porter. Cart the dead bodies about. They treat the old people like lumps of meat. When one dies they wheel him out past the others, visitors and all, and never bother to screen 'em off. When they get near to dying they usually know it and start to moan all day. A queer moan and it gets on yer nerves, you have to say, "Oh shut up, you old bugger." There's no such thing as respect for the dead.

'There are two things I'd like to have bin, a racin' driver or a test pilot, but you need money for that . . .

'Once I had eight hundred pound'. We'd just done a tobacconist—I walked into a shop—I was dressed casual like a gentleman. The salesman came up to me immediately. "Yes, sir?" "I'll have that Triumph TR3," I says and took out 725 pound' out of me pocket. "Yes, sir," he says and I drove out in that Triumph . . .

'I've gotta terrible temper, so has my wife. I never start an argument in the kitchen with her in case she picks up a knife. If I ask her to do me a hard-boiled egg and she does it soft, then I lose me temper . . .

'Know how an engine works? Come here, then I'll show yer . . .'

37 THE deserted house

He takes a wad of paper out of his pocket and opens out an advertisement for an electric-blue Mercedes SL300. 'They cost four thousand quid, you know. Your old man got four thousand quid?'

Out of the window the garden is full of tangled grass and trees.

'Let's sit down. You smell as if you never sweated in yer life . . . I don't want a girl who's bin through all what I've bin through . . .' He spreads his coat over the bare boards. Outside the dawn slides over the gasworks, slips over the rubble through the window.

'I've got to go straight now. It just ain't worth it. If they catch me I do five years. So I've got a job in a scrapyard breaking up old cars. I earn twelve pound' a week. It don't go far when you've bin used to havin' a hundred pound' in yer pocket. The trouble with me is I don't really know what I want out of life except money, but I know I want money . . . Sometimes I get a real ache inside of me when I haven't driven for a long time. Then I just have to steal a car . . . I don't go in for motor-bikes any more since me mate's accident. He hit a scaffolding lorry—one of them iron pipes went through his neck. His head was rollin' in the gutter, while his body was still on the bike racin' down the North Circular . . .'

The smell of damp from the mattress against my cheek.

'Do you ever use perfume?'

'No.'

"I'll get you some.'

At five in the morning a bird sang a complicated song.

'That's a thrush,' he says. 'I don't love my wife because I wasn't her first—she went with another bloke when she was sixteen.' He combs his hair and I look at the early morning sun dappling the filth.

DINNER hour

THE CLACKERTY-CLACK of clogs down the stone stairs of McCrindle's and out into the road in white overalls and white turbans, blinking in the hot sun.

'See him.' Sylvie catches my arm. 'His tart's up the spout,' and she holds up her hand with four fingers stretched. 'Four months she was carrying on with her best mate's old man.'

'Coming over the café for dinner?'

'Hang on while I put me shoes on.' Sylvie sits down on the steps and takes her high heels out of her bag. The hard little balls of her ankles are black with dirt. Her feet are thin in the cheap shoes one size too big. We saunter across to the packed café.

'What you want? Egg and chips? I'll get them. Go and keep them two places.'

I push my way through and sit down in the corner next to two old girls.

'Me husband deserted me twenty-nine years ago when my baby was a month old. Now I've just met up with someone else, so I went up the courts and asked if I could presume me husband dead, but they made me pay thirty shillings to look up his death certificate and they couldn't find one, so I had to apply for a divorce. The judge asked me why I'd waited twenty-nine years to apply and I told him—I was ever so embarrassed—that I'd just got another young man interested in me and he said, "That's a very good reason," and he give me a divorce.'

'You know, I did work as a washer-up in Price's canteen before I come here, but I got pleurisy on the chest from constant splashing me bosom.'

Sylvie comes back with the dinners. I spear the fat chips and dip them into the runny yolk. 'Put on a record,' and she chucks sixpence across the green glass table.

A moment later the room is drowned: 'I'm at the point of no return—for me there is no turning back!'

Sylvie leans across the table on her elbows. 'They played this at June's wedding and I had a row with Ray. He says to me, "I can't abear that when I see blokes getting hold of you." I was only having a dance with Dick and Ray says to me, "I suppose Dick's taking you home?" Well, Dick's a bit of a stirrer, a bit randy and all that, so anyway I turns to Dick and says, "Dick are you taking me home?" "No," he says, "but I'd like to," and Ray went mad. Now Ray hasn't bin down for three nights—he'll come down as soon as he wants a bit of the other. I'm not having any of that—I'll

find meself another bloke, might even look up randy Dick.'
I laugh.

'No,' says Sylvie, 'straight—if I have it once I want it three
or four times. Let's face it, you get a bit irritated seeing
the same man all the time, it's boring. Remember I got married when I was sixteen. Now I've got rid of him I like to be
out and about. I mean I've sat in watching telly for the last
five years—he even used to time me when I run round the
corner for a quarter of tea. Trouble is I can see that Ray
turning out the same if I go and live with him.'

Rube comes towards our table carrying a slopping cup of
tea.

'Hello, Rube, what happened to you last night?'

'I ended up with that Johnny back of the bombed site. He
was so worked up he got this terrible pain in his stomach. He
says I'm too hot-blooded.'

'That Jim told me he'd give me a flat and ten pound' a
week,' says Sylvie. 'Told me he loved me! "What d'you think
I am? Some high-class brass?" I says. You know he's married?'

'He's had more girls than hot dinners, he has.'

'This bloke what was with Slim—fabulous bloke he was—
says to me, "You're married, ain't you?" And I says, "Yes,
I've bin married six years." "Well," he says, "you know what
it's for then!" Cheeky bastard!'

'They always say it's the married ones what are the dirty
ones.'

'Same with Ted. I'd know if he was going out with a bird
because he'd go and get his hair done—he'd have a blow-
wave put in and all lacquer put on it and when he come

home he'd lie on the bed and say, "Now don't you dare touch it!" Then he'd have a wash and he'd use my talc and my deodorant and make me scrub his back—and all the time he'd try and keep me chained to the telly.'

'He didn't succeed, though, did he?'

Sylvie laughs. 'Remember Freddy and his ten-ton lorry? He used to wait at the end of the road for me the nights Ted went to the dogs.'

'It's better to marry an ugly man what's got good ways than a good-looker what's sly.'

We walk across the road to the factory yard. One of the boys is riding a motor-bike round in small circles. The exhaust makes wavy patterns in the still air. The women sit on the steps watching some of the men play football. Little tufts of yellow flowers push through the dusty-smelling concrete.

'Remember when me mum made us join the Salvation Army, Rube?'

'Deep and wide . . . deep and wide.' They both start singing, swaying from side to side, Sylvie in filthy old shoes and pink shirt smelling of butter, Rube, her stack of black hair on top of her head, in her tight floral get-up. 'There's a river deep and wide.'

'See that woman over there?' says Sylvie. 'She's got a finger in all the screws in Battersea and off she goes. "Anyone want any cheap underwear, birdseed, French letters, boxing gloves?" She handles just about every kind of merchandise.'

We sit on the warm concrete, leaning back against the wall, smoking.

'We had this woman from the WVS come to tell us what

to do if they dropped the H-bomb on us. "First thing," she says: "fill your bath with water." "We haven't got no bath, love," I says. That put her right in it.'

'Think I could get a job in that WVS?' says Rube. 'I fancy a change.' She stretched her bare white legs out in the sun.

'You—they wouldn't have you.'

'Why not?'

'You're not a lady.'

'A mate of mine has a good job, cinema usherette,' says Pauline, joining us. 'She finds all sorts of things when she's clearing up—nylon underwear, stockings—she even found a pair of brassières once what fitted her.'

'Listen to this then.' Old May leans across to us. 'I was cleaning in a stocking and underwear shop and me mate, Lil, was in a chemist. "You get all the stockings," she said, "and I'll get the soaps and perfumes." So I get three pairs in them cellophane packets and I stuffed them down in me front, so when I get on the bus I'm crackling like I was on fire and I see a man looking at me, so I says, "Oh, I've got terrible rheumatism and that's the cellophane to keep the fermagistine in." "Poor lady," he says.'

Flecks of soot, large as pennies, float down in the hot afternoon.

'What you doing tonight, Rube?'

'I've got a date with two ginks in a van, but I'm not going.'

'Why not?'

'Can't be bothered. Has Dave kissed yer yet?'

'No.'

'You want to get hold of him. This is Dave.' She runs her fingers up and down my legs. 'Look, she's getting all worked up. Aren't Chelsea blokes sexy?'

'No,' says Sylvie. 'They lost their knackers in the Flood.'

'What I always say is, it's not what you do, it's what you get caught doing,' says old May.

'Listen to May. Know what she gives her husband for his tea? Two threepenny-halfpenny meat-pies. She runs them under the cold tap to make them swell up. He won't be much good to yer on that, May.'

'Ah, well, life's not much without a giggle.'

SUNDAY morning

'Hurry up then. Matron's waiting for you lot to go off to church.'

'What about Moira?'

'She's stopping behind. Matron went off at her, says her baby isn't due for another fortnight and what was she making all the fuss about? "You Coloured girls should be grateful to be here at all with what goes on out in Africa," she says.'

The girls troop up the hill slowly, as some are eight or nine months gone and others have only just given birth.

'I never once lay down with him. I used to meet him in a back alley off the Latchmere. I didn't really know what he was at—I never got no pleasure out of it. I didn't know I was carrying till I was five months. I couldn't believe it—I kept thinking it would pass off. He wasn't half handsome, that's why I went with him. All the girls used to say, "What a handsome chap!" '

'Well, one thing's for sure. I'm not going steady no more. I'm going to sort meself out some one-night fellas with plenty of money.'

'Every bloke starts off as a one-night fella till you get involved.'

'We was love-struck, we didn't care what happened, and then when I found out I was carrying I couldn't abear him.'

'Moira reckoned she hadn't bin with any man—reckoned it came through the post I suppose!'

Sonia and Marion are left behind to mind the babies wrapped tight in their calico-sling cribs. The fridge and store cupboards are locked so they can't make a cup of tea, but Marion has a tin of condensed milk which she punctures with a nappy pin. They sit close together over the gas fire and take turns to suck at the hole.

Marion combs out her long hair. 'I'm not like you. I've always had worries, so I'm used to it. Anyway I was having a good time till I started to get fat at about four months. Then I tried to get rid of it, but it was too late—I never thought I might not be able to get rid of it.'

Upstairs in the dormitory Moira lies quietly moaning to herself.

Sonia holds up a photo. 'That's Mick and that's the Nissen hut in Kent—belonged to his aunt—where we stayed when we was hopping. We went down there on his motor-bike. Mick was sleepin' on a put-you-up in the kitchen. When we was all in bed I goes to get a glass of water and Mick catches hold of me legs and pulls me down—I'm lying there on top of him in me nightie and he's in the nude only covered by the sheet . . .'

'Did you feel sexy?' Marion sucks violently at the nearly empty tin.

'Not much I didn't! And then I began to wonder what I was savin' meself up for.'

'Here—it'll be nice to be looked at again, won't it? I'm going to make meself a new dress—tighter than tight, like a second skin!'

'Yeah, trouble is I couldn't somehow fancy any other fella. I s'pose it's because I've still got Mick on me mind. Course, he was extravagant—spent all his money buying gadgets for his motor-bike. That's what me mum didn't like. She kept on at me: "When are yer getting engaged? Saved enough to put down on yer bedroom suite yet?" '

Marion chucks the empty tin skilfully into the basket.

'Here I'm going to try on that new dress of Carol's while she's at church, see if I've got me figure back.'

'Me mum kept needling me—"You've got something wrong with yer stomach, Sonia, ain't yer?" " What are yer talking about, Mum?" "You look to me as if you might be carrying." "Don't be so wicked, Mum!" I'd really go off at her . . .'

Marion stands in her bra and petticoat. 'I'm not bad-lookin', am I?' She stares in the long mirror. The winter sun glints on the glass.

Sonia hunches nearer the gas. 'The worst part was tellin' me mum. "You," she said, "of all people!" She didn't expect it of me because I was such a prude at the plays on the telly. Then she told me dad and he came into me bedroom and told me not to worry. We never used to talk about that kind of thing but now we can talk about anything. Me dad went up the chemist and tried to get a stick of something they used before the war . . .'

'Thing is one can't always be scheming. Them what are always planning and scheming don't live, do they?' Marion holds her bare white arms in the air. 'I'd never take me clothes off in front of a man.'

'But they say it's marvellous when yer naked.'

'Yeah, me mate what got married told me if yer take everything off, even yer bra, and yer get between the sheets and he takes all his things off too . . .'

'That's the thing about getting married, you can have it like that every night.'

'You just lie in bed, moonlight comin' in through the window . . .' Marion shivers and climbs into the dress.

'If you love a boy and you want to give him the best thing in the world, there's only one thing, isn't there?'

'Sonia, listen!'

From upstairs screams ripped across the smug Sunday quiet. 'Moira!' She was standing by the bed barefooted on the glazed tile floor, screaming while the baby's head emerged.

Sonia ran up the hill towards the church—she hadn't bothered to put on a coat. Black water splashed up her bare legs. She sweated while her hands and feet froze.

Marion tried to make Moira lie down, but she stood stiff and screaming till the black baby slipped out with a soft thud onto the stone floor, then she collapsed.

When Matron arrived she phoned for an ambulance and covered Moira with a blanket, but she left the baby on the floor. The ambulance men wrapped it up and took it away with Moira.

At tea Matron said, 'I don't want any of you to worry about Moira's baby—it must have been dead before it was born.'

The next day two policemen arrived. Matron took them into her office. Five minutes after, the girls watched out of the window as they walked away down the garden path and nobody ever saw black Moira again.

WEDDING anniversary

THE SWEET smell of cow-cake from Garton's blows up the road with the violet smoke from the Power Station. 'I think if you don't reckon someone it drives you mad if they're jealous, but if you think something of a bloke you like him to be a bit possessive.' Sylvie and I walk up the summer evening road to the Prodigal. An old lady in slippers comes out of the off-licence with a zip bag weighing her sideways. From open windows the telly calls. 'But Ted—he used to time me when I slipped round the corner to put a bet on for me dad . . . I was the youngest bride in Battersea, married at fifteen, had Mike when I was fifteen-and-a-half. Ten minutes after he was born I was sittin' up in bed suckin' a stick of rock.'

Down the street women stand at their doors and two young

girls walk hippity-hop on their high heels, eating fish and chips.

'Expected me to live in a furnished room in Brixton. What could I do in one room all day. If you've got two, at least you can go from one to the other. Didn't even like me going early-morning cleaning with me mum, so then he starts going to the dogs every Wednesday night and I meet up with this Fred, handsome fella! Every Wednesday in his ten-ton truck, waitin' on the corner. Cor . . .'

Along the pavement the children play in an echo of names, Johnny, Moraine, Dawn and Sherry.

'In the winter he'd leave the engin' runnin'. Phew, it didn't half get hot stuck up in that cabin and the vibratin'— Cor . . . Come on, let's shoot in here.' We push through the swing doors into the pub and pause a moment to case the Saturday-night joint before it closes in around us.

'My baby was born Friday. A son it was. I'm glad it's a boy, I'll soon teach him to steal. Wait till he's nine or ten, then send him out pinching while I sit back.'

'What yer going to do till he's nine or ten?'

'I'll send me wife out on the game.'

'You wouldn't do that.'

'I would, I'd send me mother too.'

'He would too, if anybody would have her,' says Sylvie, licking the brown foam around her lips.

The boys close in. 'Excuse me, but with that dress it's difficult to stop me eyes wandering.'

'Well, as long as yer hands don't wander, mate.'

'I was cleaning the windows in some posh flats in Kensington and the lady in there started chatting me up and says, would I do her bedroom last as she's got to get changed? So when I comes to the bedroom I starts polishing away and then she sits down and starts taking off her stockings right under me nose. "Just got a ladder," she says. The next week she rings up the firm: "Will you please be sure to send the same man because he was very satisfactory." '

'Oh yeah, got a recommendation from the aristocracy—you must be all right then.'

In the corner Mrs Hardy and her old cronies hold court. 'Here, you know old Taylor died. He was a woman-hater, that old man, a bachelor all is life—I don't believe he so much as spoke to a woman if he could help. Then last week he goes and dies. There I was clearin' out his drawers for him—he didn't have no family—and I came across this huge collection of dirty postcards. Never seen anything like it. "Woman-hater indeed," I said, "he was kiddin' all of us!" '

'Where yer going on your holidays, Fat Lil?'

'I always go up to see me sister in Nottingham. We get drunk arse over head out of the pub every night.'

Their laughter rattles through the beery room.

'I go and stay with me daughter, it costs me bugger-all. They take one of them caravans. Last year I was sitting out in the bloody front in a deck-chair and I sees me little granddaughter and I'm laughing so much I goes right through the bloody canvas, legs in the air, and I split me trousers!' Again the old women laugh. Fat Lil stamps her old feet, blue veins bulging out of broken shoes.

The piano bangs out and the singer holds a pint of cold beer in one hand and the mike in the other and croons, 'If you was the only girl in the world and I was the only boy.'

His eyes water and he sets his cap at a still more jaunty angle.
'There would be such wonderful things to do . . .'

Now the pub is packed. Cheap serge suits press against you
as someone tries to get past.

'Up on Clapham Common there's a place under a dip
called Frying Pan Alley. Wanta come and see?'

'Oh, don't say things like that, you make me itch all over.'
Sylvie laughs, sticking her tongue out of the corner of her
mouth. 'Ask Jeanie to go up there with you. I knocked for
her seven o'clock this morning to go to work. When I opens
the door she was lying back in her black nylon night-dress.
"You on yer honeymoon or something?" I says.'

'Come on, Sylvie, get up on the mike!'

Sylvie stands on the wooden platform. She holds one hand
in the air palm outwards and sings, 'You're as sweet as a
rose in June, dear, I love you, adore you, I do . . .' She turns
her hand in circles, her short fingers showing broken nails.
'Out of the blue skies the dark clouds come rollin', breaking
my heart in two . . .'

Johnny puts his hand inside my coat. 'I guess you're not
like those women in the ads what you see giving their husbands a meal, serving it up and worrying all the time how
they're going to get the washing up done. I guess you're more
casual, isn't that right?'

The air is thick with smoke and beer. Out of the window
the sky is blazing pink as the sun goes down behind the four
chimneys.

'What yer doing tomorrow?' he asks.

'Havin' a bath.'

'Is it your birthday then?'

'Cheek!'

'Like to come to a party tonight?'

'What sort of a party?'

'A weddin' anniversary!'

'All right. We'll see you round there in half an hour.'

'Here, look at 'im!' Fat Lil takes a paper cut-out of a little man out of her pocket and goes around the pub, showing him to all. 'I bet I know what you'll be dreaming of tonight!' She moves him up and down.

'You don't have to dream when you've got the real thing, love.' Mrs Hardy shouts with laughter. 'Nature calls me sometimes. I hear the call of nature. I may be a bit wheezy, but I'm still livin'.'

We pile out laughing onto the pavement and, clutching one another, roll down to the fish-shop for some skate and chips. The fish is hot and slippery between my hungry fingers. Sylvie squats behind a ten-ton truck for a piss and the truck moves off and she's left screaming in the road. 'Here, wait till I've pulled me drawers up!'

Round the corner, past the half-destroyed building of the Savoy cinema and behind an erection, a tower with bright red letters: BOOTH'S GIN.

'Here, look at that old bloke laying in the gutter. We'd better turn him over in case it's me dad.'

Now the stars are out as we turn into Reform Street. A crowd of them tumble out of the bright doorway of a house and among them is Ted and he sees Sylvie and he stands cocky and arrogant among his friends. 'Where d'you think you're going all dressed up like the Queen of Sheba?'

'What's that to you—you fifth-rate ponce?'

They face each other in the gentle air. Everyone is quiet and Ted staggers and quivers with drink and rage. 'You ferkin' whore, I know you had that abortion round the corner fer ten quid, I can prove it!'

Sylvie goes for him. He hits her, she screams in anger and someone tries to pull her back. He hits her again and she falls down. 'You ferkin' brute and you don't give nothin' to your son!'

'I give him two shirts!'

An old man standing by shouts, 'Yes, she deserves a beatin', she's not worth a light. They're all the the same!' Sylvie swings round and jumps upon him punching and hitting till he falls to the ground. 'Sylvie, not an old man!' a woman screams. People watch from their windows, and down the street men have come out of the pubs and stand under the gas-lamps silently.

'I know you went with a ferkin' prostitute. You still owe her three pound' for yer pleasure, that bleeding tart what went and got herself killed. Wish it had bin you what had got killed.'

'I know all about that abortion you had and whose bleedin' kid it was and all.'

The gas-lamps with the chipped silver mosaics round their brims spilling out light across a strip of waste, a bent pram and the iron guts of a motor-car. The pubs are open till midnight because Princess Margaret got married today.

'Leave yer wife alone!'

'She ain't no wife of mine. I had to marry her, didn't I? She was havin' a kid.'

'I wish I'd never married yer.'

And now round the corner, clutching her old brown coat around her, hobbles Mum. 'What's going on then?' Teddy stands on the corner, cocky hands on hips.

'You ferkin' . . .' She takes off her coat and rushes at him in her long night-gown, her mottled arms all bare. 'You hit my kid, you bugger . . .' Her wild black hair stands up as she flails out wildly. 'Now you hit me, you just hit me, you dirty fucker!' She whacks him across the ear, then stands back taunting him: 'You dirty coward . . .'

Down the hill glides a police car and the crowd melts into the shadows. Four men jump out.

'It was nothing, Inspector. Come on, we're just on our way home!'

'What are you doing in yer night-dress, Mother?' The Inspector grins after us as we troop up the warm road.

'Never mind, Sylvie.'

Sylvie pushes her blond hair back behind her ear. 'Keep never-minding, it's only fer life.'

THE clipjoint

"As FROM tonight girls please take NOTICE. That your dress in general will be checked each night also your hair. Remember you have to sit with the customers so *please* be CLEAN." Signed Sonny, written in biro on a torn bit of cardboard and stuck to the cloakroom mirror. It was eight o'clock in the evening. We hurried in and signed our names in the book, Rena, Jeanie, Mary, Dawn, Moraine and Georgie. 'First come, first served'—the name at the top of the list gets the first customer.

Rena, a thin girl from Poplar in a brown jersey suit with a green sequined neckline, had taken me under her wing. 'You've just got to kid 'em along, love, you'll soon learn.' We were crammed in a tiny room among empty paint tins and stiff brushes. On the wall a rusty perfume machine 'Exotique, Aimant . . .' and a dirty mirror which Moraine rubs vigorously with her hand and then peers hopefully into, blueing her dark-rimmed eyes. Sonny sticks his Irish head round the door and looks at me—'I want to see yer in the office when yer ready.'

'Go on then, but say yer busy if he asks you up for a drink tomorrow afternoon—they reckon he's clapped up to the eye-balls.'

The office is behind the bar, an alcove partitioned off by a curtain. 'Your job is to get the customers in—entice 'em a bit. I'll leave it to your own discretion just what you tell 'em but jockey 'em along in the hopes of a floorshow or strip-tease.'

'How much do you hope to take a night?'

'About a hundred pound', but fifty of that goes to the girls, then I've got five touts to pay. Oh yes, I've got the tout on the door and four out around London searching for likely customers. Then there's me rent and the waitress—by the time that's all paid up it only leaves me with a bare living.'

We distributed ourselves around the room, leaning back, legs crossed on the red serge settees. I sat next to Rena. 'I've got a kid of nine. I'd never let him suffer for anyone but I had to let me mum have him because I was down in the basement and he'd sit up every night howling his eyes out till I got back.'

The peroxide waitress, a retired brass from Stepney, starts sweeping the floor with a huge broom. 'Mind yer legs, girls.' Sonny follows her round with a giant container of deodorant spray and fills the air with a thick numbing solution. Rena takes a gold chain out of a crumpled paper bag. 'See this, it's real gold—I gave a tenner for it, you can have it for five.'

The buzzer rang twice. 'That's two customers coming up.' Rena and Jeanie make for the curtained doorway. Two sheepish looking Indians peer in. Rena sticks her arm through the first one. 'Come and sit down, sir.'

'Orchestra? We wanted orchestra.'

'The orchestra's coming later, they got held up.' She pulled him into the gloom while he gently resisted. 'This way, sir, I'll get you a drink,' said tall Jeanie to the delicate Indian at her side.

'No thank you, I think we go.'

Eight vampish girls stare at the men from the rosy haze of the otherwise empty room.

'Not now you can't go—not now you've come this far. You'll have to pay your ten bob entrance fee.'

'What don't you like about it anyway?'

'We wanted orchestra—'

'I've told you the orchestra's coming.'

'Now give us ten bob each and then you can buy a drink.'

The first Indian fumbled in his pocket and gave a pound to Rena. 'We can go now?'

'Yeah, get out.'

They hurried out. We could hear them clattering rapidly down the concrete stairs.

'I could tell they were rubbish directly they looked in.'

'How long you bin here, Rena?'

'Eleven years. I started clubbing when I was seventeen. You kind of get addicted. I always think the next man that walks through that door may be my opposite number.'

Sonny fiddled with the juke-box, which suddenly burst

forth 'Rambling Rose, Rambling Rose, Why she rambles no one knows . . .'

'I've bin here nine years and I've never had a customer ask me to marry him. I've had 'em ask me plenty of other things but never that,' said red-haired Georgie.

'Well, she might be better off—you never know your luck —specially not down here. You get all kinds of cranks.'

Things were pretty dead except for occasional scuffles at the entrance. 'Come and sit down, sir. You needn't stay if you don't want to, sir. What don't you like about the place, you're not even inside really.' And the curtains sway violently. 'You don't like the look of me, don't yer—well pay yer entrance fee and piss off.' Then just after eleven the pubs shut and suddenly things livened up. The buzzer buzzed wildly three-four-five times.

I hurried to the curtains close behind Moraine's sequin-swathed bottom. Three yellowish gentlemen appeared and blinked nervously in the dim light. First Dawn and then Moraine pinioned their choice by the arm. I was left with the fat one. 'Would you like to come and sit down?' Gingerly I plucked at his sleeve. 'Yes.' I led the way to the table next to his friends and sat myself down. He crashed down next to me, his haunch against mine. The waitress appeared. 'Ten shillings entrance fee and would you like to buy the young lady a drink?' She plonked two glasses of coloured water down in front of me without waiting for his reply. He took out his wallet. 'Shandy for you, sir, or ginger beer?'

'Whisky?'

'No, sir, no licence, I'll get you a shandy. That'll be one

pound fourteen and six with your entrance fee.' He paid up and then he turned to me and silently looked me up and down.

'Where do you come from?'

'Brazilia.'

There was a long pause, his eyes bulge and then, 'Please excuse me but I would like to make love with you.'

'Could you ask one of the other girls, I'm not very good at it.'

'No,' he said, 'it would be better for you if you would know Brazilian love and experience'—he placed a pudgy hand on my thigh.

I look around and see Rena tickling her customer under the chin.

I jumped up.

'Get back there and kid him along—NIT!' says Rena.

Slowly I returned. 'Well,' I said, 'what about me coming round to your hotel when I've finished here?'

'No good, thirty of my company share hotel with me.'

He felt in his pocket and got out seven and sixpence. 'I want to see you in the colour of your skin.'

'That's the colour of my skin.' I pointed to my naked shoulder.

'No,' he said, 'there,' and he dug his finger into my thigh.

'I make curtain for you.' He lifted the edge of the table-cloth hiding my legs from view. I pulled my skirt up half an inch. He banged down the first half-crown. 'Lovely strong legs. Black stocking, are they in the mode? More!' he said, pointing to my leg. I yanked it up another inch before I noticed the retired brass standing over us. 'You want to buy the young lady another drink?'

'Okay,' he said.

She put down two in front of me. 'That'll be a pound, sir. Don't lose yer sticks, love, or you won't get any money at the end.'

He gave her the money and she poured one glass into the other and put the empty one back on the tray. 'Half a crown service, sir, please.'

'Now,' he said, 'you let me make love?'

'Well, it's a bit awkward.' He held up a ten-shilling note and dangled it before my eyes. 'Only for two hours I give you this.'

I pocketed my two half crowns from the table. 'No good, sir, I'm a nice girl.'

'All right, I go.' He stood up, his fat tummy knocking over my glass, the pink water making a little puddle on the glass table.

It was midnight. The waitress banged a cup of tea down in front of me.

Rena's customer had also left. She was by herself twisting in the middle of the room on the red and black squares of erupting lino. A voice wailed, 'Oh yes, I wanta marry you.'

Rena came over. 'Come to the toilets with me? I'm scared to go up there on me own. I might find a big black man.'

'Hopeful,' said Mary, gulping down her tea.

'What d'yer mean, hopeful?' There was a moment's tension then Rena dropped it and stalked toward the toilets.

'Two rolls that's all I've had between my lips today. Only made twenty-five bob last night.'

The lavatory was down one flight of concrete stairs. LADIES! WILL YOU PLEASE PULL THE CHAIN!

'What's at the bottom of the stairs?'

'A shoe factory—if you're ever really pushed for a place, it's private but you've gotta stand.'

We went back to the dim smoky room and waited by the curtains for the next customers.

'Four of us girls share a cab back to Poplar—if yer going that way—'

The buzzer went. Rena hitched up her bra and opened the curtains. 'Good evening, sir.' 'Is there a floor show?'

'About one o'clock, sir.'

'Where are they going to perform, on top of the juke-box?'

'Don't be sarcastic, sir—you've got lovely hair.'

She led him on into the dim room. Dawn came hurtling through the curtains. 'I went out to his car with him. He said he had a Rolls but it was only a rotten little Mini—big phony. I jumped out at the lights. He gave me a cheque for twenty pound'. Do you think it's any good?'

Johnny, the youngest tout with blue mac and blue circles under his eyes, comes in with six men straight from the Raymond Revue bar sexed up to the ears.

'I'm in the motor-car industry—business is very bad, the proles won't buy cars.'

'I want something hot, you're too cold.'

'Georgie, yer regular's here.' A man with an open-necked shirt and a flash camera came in. 'Hello, Georgie love, how's business?' Rena hisses in my ear, 'I like 'em all as long as they're nice-looking.'

I sit down with my man. 'My father was a beachcomber in Bermuda—he wasn't coloured or anything, actually he was born in Park Lane. My great-grandfather owned the Grosvenor Hotel, that's what put our family in the money. Can we go back to your place?'

Next door I heard Rena at work, 'Make this one the last, sir? Come on, just one last one.' 'No, you've had four in the last half hour.' 'Please yerself.' She gets up and leaves him to drink his lukewarm shandy on his own. He takes a last sip, screws up his face and leaves.

Then two young Norwegian sailors, just been paid off from an oil tanker. Mine wasn't more than eighteen with no tie and a frayed shirt buttoned up to the neck. His cropped hair was a whitish blond and his eyes red-rimmed. The waitress hovered over him with her tin tray full of the tiny glasses of coloured water and a bit of orange peel stuck through with a stick. She could see he was young and a sucker. 'Buy the young lady a drink?' She put four glasses in front of me. 'That'll be two pounds.' He took out a small bundle of dirty notes. 'And a tip for the waitress?'

At half past two Sonny turned on four 100-watt bulbs and the men covered their eyes with hot hands.

'Into the cloakroom, girls.' Once again we squeezed into the tiny room. The girls put on their headscarves and macs and leant against the wall.

'Oh, me eyes aren't half sore.'

'I reckon you've got the conjunctivitis.'

'What's that?'

'An infection.'

'Infection? I haven't got no infection—where d'you think I've bin to get an infection?'

I made to leave. 'Don't go out there or Sonny will never get rid of the men.'

'How much you done, love?'

'Never mind, might do better tomorrow—'

At last we were let out. Sonny put the notes in little bundles on the bar and we lined up. The touts sat around on the stained settees bantering the girls. 'Don't forget yer mudpack, Moraine.' 'Remember yer appointment for the face-lift.'

The waitress brushed up cigarette ends from the tattered carpet. Jeanie helped collect the shredded paper napkins, green, pink and blue, torn and crumpled in frustration.

'Oh gawd, I've got the backache and I'm meeting a customer at half past three. He'll have to send me home in a cab.'

Sonny tossed each girl's sticks in a tin lid to check the numbers and then paid out.

'Well, how d'yer find yer first night?' said Rena. 'The great thing in this life is you can choose—to do or not to do —if you get my meaning—at least we're free!'

BANG on the common

THE LITTLE slum house was locked and in darkness. A voice came out of the night: 'Are you looking fer Winny?'

'Oh, hello, Annie.'

'Oh, it's you, Rube.'

The three of us stood under the dim gas-light. 'She bought a big place out at Wimbledon bang on the Common. As it happens, I'm just going to phone her up. A flash tart in a big motor came down looking for her today—said if I'd find Winny and get her done for ten she'd give me a couple of quid for meself.'

'Who's it for, you or her?'

'A mate in work.'

'Come off it, Rube. I won't blacken yer character.'

'Oh, all right. It's me, Annie. I think I'm up the spout. I can't seem to sit still. I can't stay in for nothing. I've got to be movin' around the whole time. I can't eat nothing. Directly I start to eat I feel full.'

'Sounds like yer in the club all right.'

'I can't have it done. I might get an air-bubble in me inside and die. I walked out on me job today, I'm all on edge. I'd run away but I've nowhere to run to.'

'You'd best have it done. You're only a kid, she'd do it for five quid.'

'I said to the doctor, "I've bin going with a fella and you know how it happens." "Yes," he says.'

'You'd best go up to Winny's and have done with it. I *could* get you some quinine. I took some once. There was a loud ringing in me ears and a violent pain in me stomach, it lifted me into another world—but it didn't do no good. This Barry, he gets it from the chemist. Tells him he's got a mate just back from Africa with a touch of the malaria, then he sells the tablets ten bob each to the girls.'

Rube was cheerful now the first move had been made. 'Will you phone her for me, Annie?'

'Yeah. When do yer want to go?'

'Tomorrer. When me mum's in the kitchen I have to take a deep breath and hold me stomach in and run past, then when I get out into the scullery I let it out. She said to me today. "You got ulcers in yer mouth? Your stomach must be upset" and she gave me one of her looks.'

The next evening we took a bus up to Wimbledon. A long street with rows of red-brick villas. The three of us traipse along the road.

'I thought it was bang on the Common, Annie.'

'Well, it's near enough.' She stopped at a corner house with a hardware store in front. 'So she's got a shop and all.'

'Yeah, it's her sideline.' We went in.

'Hello, darling. Hello, love.' Winny was about forty-five. She wore a red dress above her knees showing her varicose-vein legs, ankle socks and gym shoes.

'I had that Harry here again last night. He didn't go till six this morning. I made him sleep in the bath. He's bringing me fifty gal's of paint tomorrer—free sample.' "Well," I says to him, "you've had my free sample, now what about yours?" ' She had delicate arms and huge bony hands with long red fingers which she waved around.

'Well, what have we here, Annie?'

'I've come, I've come . . .' said Rube, nervous.

'I know why you've come—there's only one reason good-looking girls come to see Winny. Here, Annie, pop across the off-licence and get me a quarter-bottle whisky.' She gave her a ten-shilling note and Rube and I were left alone with Winny.

'How far are you gone, love?'

'About three months.'

Winny poked Rube in the stomach. 'Oh, then you've only got a small problem in there.'

'You see I can't keep it . . .' Rube began.

'Don't try and explain, love. How can you ever explain anything? It's the most bloody impossible thing in the world. How much money have you got?'

'Four pounds.'

'Give it over. You don't look more than seventeen.'

'I'm eighteen next month.'

'Come on upstairs, then your friend can wait for you down here.'

But that wasn't the last time Rube and I trailed up to Wimbledon. She had to go seven times before anything happened. Often we'd go into the kitchen and Winny would be sitting on some man's knee. As Rube said, 'She wouldn't care if you was watching her—teasin' 'em, sloppin' over 'em.' Winny didn't eat anything all day. She was always on the bottle.

Later I'd cart Rube home weak-kneed and trembling on the bus. 'Terry came down for me last night—the first time in six weeks. He said, "Don't you go up there no more, I don't want no kid of mine to go down the drain." But Sylvie said, "Now she's started she's gotta keep on or it'll be born a monster." So Terry walks out, but not before he shouted so half the street can hear: "Anyway she was nothing but a cheap thrill." '

We rode past the park. The water lilies are opening red mouths. The birds hop in the flower garden and the crazy music streams from the fairground.

'When she does the syringe you feel a sort of weakening pain shoot up in yer . . .'

It was about six on a Sunday morning. There was a banging on my door. I looked out of the window and saw Johnny Macarthy below. I knew it must be serious because Johnny deserted from the army fifteen years ago and hadn't been outside his own house since in case they caught up with him—so far they hadn't.

I let him in out of the dark mist, 'It's Rube. She's ever so bad. I want to phone up Winny.'

Johnny phoned Winny. It rang a long time and when she finally answered it she said she couldn't come.

I went back over with Johnny. Rube was lying back against her mum's knees, a green eiderdown covering her, white and heaving.

'Let me get the doctor.'

'No, they might try and save the baby. I don't want no kids from that gink—we've enough kids in this house as it is without no more.'

'I told her, didn't I, to keep away from him?' said her mum.

A few hours later Rube started to shriek. Her jet-black hair stuck to her face and tiny rivulets of blue rinse coursed down her white cheeks. She was semi-delirious.

The smell of Sunday dinner cooking floated up the stairs. Rube bent up tight with pain.

'It's lucky I ain't got me health and strength no more else I'd do him, do him right up I would,' said her mum. Sylvie came in. 'I'll hold her now, Mum, if you want to go and have yer dinner. Ray says he'd hit him sky-high if it wasn't that he might get nicked for it.'

The voice of Johnny, sailed up from the kitchen: 'He'd better watch it from me, too—I shan't always be stayin' in, will I?'

Rube shrieked again.

'Let me ring the doctor.'

'Oh, all right then.'

In the kitchen everyone was eating. The light was full on. Ben E. King sang:

> *Oh yes, she said, yes,*
> *And she opened her arms.*
> *Oh yes, she said, yes and*
> *She closed her eyes.*

When I came back from ringing, Rube was shrieking, a long, high, animal shriek. The baby was born alive, five months old. It moved, it breathed, its heart beat.

Rube lay back, white and relieved, across the bed. Sylvie and her mum lifted the eiderdown and peered at the tiny baby still joined by the cord. 'You can see it breathing, look!'

Rube smiled. 'It's nothing—I've had a look meself.'

'I reckon she had some pluck going seven times,' said her mum.

Finally the ambulance arrived. They took Rube away, but they left behind the baby, which had now grown cold. Later Sylvie took him, wrapped in the *Daily Mirror*, and threw him down the toilet.

WASH night

PEOPLE ARE drifting home from work. A boy rides by, a girl across his handlebars. A dog lies in the road with a bone. A motor-bike revs by the new flats.

Rube, eating a roll, comes out of her house pushing a pram piled high with dirty clothes and sheets and green- and yellow-striped towels. Sylvie follows, carrying the Daz and a bottle of bleach. 'Come on then.'

Three abreast, we push the prams up the road laughing, and Sylvie calls out to people she knows; 'Hello, me old cock.'

A shunting train hoots in the Junction as we turn onto the debris. St. Peter's red tower, high over the shambling terraces and the sewer airing post and the band of mongrel dogs sniffing over the abandoned objects.

'Hear about Tom?' says Rube. 'He walked Pat home the

other night. She wouldn't let him in the bedroom, so he nearly kicked the door in.'

'Any bloke'll try and get in the bedroom if yer mum's out. It's only natural, ain't it?'

A strong smell drifts across the evening from the cow-cake factory.

'It's not like Pat to shut a bloke out of the bedroom. Know what 'appened last week-end? Me, Pat and Millie met up with these blokes, so they asked us to come back to their flat—nice little flat it was, all done out modern—but Millie pissed off and left us, so we was two girls and three blokes—Irish blokes. Mine was called Chris. "We're sleepin' in 'ere," he says, "and Pat can sleep with the other two." Pat starts moaning. "Go on," I says, "you need two of 'em half-pint-sized blokes." Next mornin' I asked Pat where she slept. "On the outside," she says. Poor cow, she could hardly walk.'

We turn the corner, laughing, across the concrete yard and into the baths.

'Any boy you go out with, nine times out of ten you end up talking about sex.'

The huge damp room, the smell of boiled sheets in the soapy, steamy air. 'One-and-six for your coloureds, half a crown for your whites, as much as you like in the machine.' Mrs Hardy sploshes over the wet floor towards me. 'Hello, love. I had a good dinner today. I always go up and have a nice dinner Wednesday when me son gives me the toot. I had roast mutton, roast potatoes, mint sauce and cabbage and then a good bit of tart to finish up with—half a crown, that's all they charge. I don't like to cook me own dinner. It drives yer barmy, don't it, cookin' yer own dinner when yer by yerself?'

The women bend over their tubs, rubbing and scrubbing, absorbed in the work. The vast driers fling the clothes round and round. 'All right, old fruit?' Sylvie yells across the noisy room.

Rube comes over. 'Here, let me do it for yer.' She takes the brush and scrubs violently the dirt-stained jeans. 'Gettin' rid of that kid hasn't half changed me. I don't know what I want any more. I ain't half quick-tempered. I go off at everyone around me. Christmas-time I smashed all the cups off of the table . . .'

'Met a gorgeous bloke last night—the sort of bloke when you see him you want to grab hold of him . . .'

We pull the whites out of the drier and shove them through the giant presser flattening the sheets, then catching and folding as they come out.

'He kept pressin' himself against me, then his hands began to wander. "You ain't half hot-blooded," he says. I kept takin' them away, then he'd put them back again. "I can't help being sexy," I says. He works in a garage—that's how he come to have a car. He drove me out to London Airport for a snoggin' session. We sat in the front and June and his mate, Ron, were in the back. June says she'll have it with Ron if he goes steady with her first because she's bin let down that way once or twice before. My one kept on at me to get out of the car and lie on the grass with him. "S'posin' an aeroplane lands on us?" I says. I reckon he was after me crumpet . . .'

The pile of clean clothes grows higher on the scrubbed wooden table.

'Go and shove this lot in the pram while I help Sylvie.' I sit on the wooden bench to wait next to an old woman from down our street. Her breasts hang like two cheeses in a gauze bag. It is nearly eight and the women are turning off the machines and sluicing down the floor with hosepipes.

'Me daughter looked something like you,' says the old girl. 'She was only twenty-four and she died of a broken heart because of her rotten old man—he liked other women—so my husband worked to bring up her kids. I see the rain runnin' out his trouser bottoms . . . He died Sunday night. The police come and told me Monday mornin'. It was a terrible shock. They've called in me pension-book, so I only get thirty bob this week and sixteen goes on the rent. I've been trying to get together a cheap bit of black, but you can't get it. He went to a bone up there in the 'ospital. I haven't taken me clothes off for three weeks, it's the shock. I haven't bin able to clean the place up since he died.'

At eight o'clock they turn us out into the night with our loaded prams. It is drizzling now as we hurry three abreast in the middle of the road. Cars hoot at us to get out of the way.

'I think I might be carrying,' says Sylvie. 'I'm going up Hastings tomorrer to put down on a bedroom suite.'

Through a lighted window a young man, stripped to the waist, a silver chain round his neck, combs his hair.

'I nearly got raped last Sunday, but he was an old bloke and I didn't fancy him, so I didn't let him.' A train rushes by along the line above us, lighting up the sky above the

Junction. We buy some fish and chips to eat as we go. Rube
sings, 'He's got the power, he makes me do things I don't
want to doooo, he's got the power of love over meeee . . .'

'Trouble is,' says Sylvie, 'when you've bin going steady
and you've bin used to a little bit and then you break it off,
you get frustrated.'

'Well, it's no good you breakin' it off if yer in the club.'

'What am I going to do? Me mum'll do her nut if I leave
home.'

Two boys try to light a bonfire. It smoulders and catches
and they lean great doors up against it till the middle flames

and flares, a red mass in the dusky rubble, and the boys laugh and throw on more rubbish.

'I can't help being hot-blooded, can I?

Down a basement coals are burning, hot jazz is playing, and the room is thick with Coloureds.

'I reckon all our germs come from them foreigners. You don't know what they bring over with them.' Rube pushes open the broken wooden gate. 'Comin' in for a cuppa tea?'

On the floor the two children play in their underpants in front of the fire, the orange-flowered curtains are drawn, the telly in the next room is on. 'Two boys just knocked for you. Ever so nice they were. I had to tell them you was ill. I would have gone out with them meself, only I wasn't dressed,' says Mrs Macarthy.

'What d'you think they'd want to take you out for, Mum, if they come and knocked for us?'

Sylvie puts the kettle on. 'I'm going to have a scrub and go up the off-licence for some chocolate,' says Rube.

'Don't go meetin' up with that totter. I don't want you hookin' up with no totters, you never know when they're going to bring home a week's wages . . . filthy lot . . .'

'Oh shut up, Mum!'

Rube sits in a chair washing her big feet in a bowl of water.

'Here, you know that smart bloke what's moved into number sixty-one, they reckon he's a queer. "Impersonatin and importin'," that's what they calls it—you can do time for that—importin' . . .' says Mrs Macarthy. Sylvie dances about imitating the queers: 'Went to the queers' ball up the Cricketers the other night . . . wow it was a ball and all . . .

they was all winkin' at the fellas . . . dressed up in long kilts . . . cor, what a carry on . . . "Drag" they call that, you can get three years for it . . .'

'They say a lot of them's mentally disturbed . . .' Sylvie pours the hot black tea onto the tinned milk. 'Tell 'er about that job you 'ad, Mum.'

'Yeah, me friend Fat Lil says, "I've found a lovely job for you and me, ten-shilling-a-week bonus for mental efficiency." So we goes to work in this big posh place in Knightsbridge. The Supervisor says, "Whatever you do don't open the windows." Well, Fat Lil had to shake out the mats so she opens the window and in jumps a man with half his face missin' and flung himself on 'er and she falls to the ground and he's screamin', "Lips! Lips!" Fat Lil hollered blue murder and I was out and half way down Knightsbridge but I goes back later for me cards . . . it wasn't no mental efficiency we was gettin' our bonus for but mental deficiency . . .'

Mrs Macarthy doubles up laughing and coughing. 'Another time me and Fat Lil was cleanin' in some posh flats and Fat Lil see a bit of carpet. "That would look nice in me front passage," she says, and she gets out a razor blade and starts cuttin' it away from the floor. "How are you going to get it out past the hall porter?" I says. "I'll wrap it round me middle," she says, and that's what she done. She wraps it round and round and ties it with a piece of string and she has a big overcoat to the ground and she walks out past the porter. When we gets to the bus she couldn't step up the step and everyone's givin' her a hand pushin' and pullin' . . . I nearly died . . . but it looks nice in her front passage . . .'

'Like a bit of cake?' Sylvie cuts fat wedges of Madeira.

Rube takes her stockings off of the fender and pulls them over her feet.

'Got a nice frock off the barrers today. Come from some posh place over Chelsea—must have cost a few quid.' Mrs Macarthy holds up a green satin dress; 'I'll let you have it for half a crown . . .'

There's a knock at the door. 'Who is it?"

'It's June.'

Rube stands in the passage by the open door. Their conversation wafts towards the kitchen.

'I can't go with him . . . he's too short. He's a very decent fella and all that but he's too short . . .'

'Ain't it funny you going with the driver . . . I usually go with the driver . . .'

Bert comes into the kitchen. 'Let's have a cuppa tea then.' 'Make it yerself.'

'Don't come it with me, Cummy Lil.' Sylvie replies by hitting him over the head with the sauce bottle.

Rube and June have disappeared towards the off-licence. I walk across the road.

Mrs Hardy leans on her gate in the gloaming. 'Hello, love, just gettin' a breath of air after me bacon puddin'. I had a lodger for thirteen years. He was a very greedy man and I gave him bread puddin' and bacon puddin' for his tea and he dropped down dead. So I went along to tell his daughter. "He's just dropped dead!" Of course I didn't tell her about the bacon puddin'. "What have yer done with his clothes?" she says. "You're not havin' them," I says, "what about me rent?" So I takes them round to the rag man and I got twelve shillings and I buys meself a quarter of whisky and a packet of fags . . . I had a drop of whisky what me brother gave me last night and I meant to save the rest for Christmas and then I thought well I mightn't be here for Christmas . . .'

Later as I go to bed I hear a raucous voice blowing across the street on the late night breeze.

'Standing outside the door with yer coat all undone for quarter of an hour saying good night—I told you I don't want no totters down here . . .'

And Rube's voice shouting back. 'The alley don't belong to you, it's a public convenience ent it?'

OUT with the boys

THE HOT egg spilt into the bread as I bit hungrily. 'There's only two things money can't buy, love and life. I think an awful lot of you.' His long fingers, ingrained with dirt, stretched around the steamy mug.

We were in a transport café on an arterial road. A gang of boys came in with eagles on their backs and TRIUMPH painted beneath in luminous white letters. One of them wore a shirt spotted with blood, his hand wrapped in a blood-soaked towel. They greeted one another by a toss of the head.

'I was working in Ford's and I started nicking the cars straight off the production line. They was all complete except for their number plates—they'd park them out in a field behind the factory. I'd just drive them away and sell 'em for spare parts. I got two years in a Yorkshire Borstal. I was running four or five rackets in there—bookmaking, toilet requisites. I'd only been with this girl four times when I got nicked. I didn't know she was pregnant till I was away. She come up to Yorkshire and they married us in the chapel. I only saw her for an hour in the waiting-room. Now I've got a son called Shane. She goes off at me for going out. I suppose we just don't get on. She's got long hair right down her back. I like long hair.'

Over the far side of the café long-distance drivers ground the crushed straws into the black floor with the toes of their boots and poured sauce on huge plates of egg and chips.

A couple of girls lolled against the pulsing juke-box—'Oh, Carol, I'm so in love with you,' their loose blond hair dangling over imitation leather coats and their make-up in little plastic bags.

Terry came over. 'I'm in trouble, I hit a policeman— chinned him. He was messin' me about, pushin' me around on the pavement, so I chinned him, didn't I? Then I run, but he come after me with another one and they dragged me up to the station. Look at me back!' He pulled his sweater up and we saw the blue marks across his ice-white skin. Another boy joined us. 'I used to drive the Big Dipper, but I got the sack. I was drunk and I knocked a ferkin' cripple off the line—he was mending it. He was only a ferkin' cripple—couldn't get out of the way in time.'

'Well, he'd have probably got done in by the H-bomb if you hadn't killed him.'

'Have you heard about this four-minute lark? There's this Geneva Convention where they've agreed to phone up four minutes before they send off a rocket to give the other blokes a chance to prepare themselves.'

'Yeah, but once one bomb explodes it starts off a whole chain of bombs exploding Norway, France—all over the place.'

'They give us a lecture at the end of the National Service: what to do if an H-bomb dropped. At eight hundred yards and over yer all right if you lie flat on yer face and cover all yer bare skin, then the radiation will pass over you.'

A road-floosie stood drinking, eyes rimmed dark and short shaggy hair. She wore an old jumper and a black skirt, her legs a dirty white, and high black shoes. She smiled, both hands round the white mug, and laughed with the men as she sipped the scalding tea.

'Put a record on.' He spun me a sixpence across the table and I got up.

'That's a posh pair of swanky ankles someone's got.' A boy came up behind me. 'Take me home with you tonight.'

'My mother'll be there.'

'I'll give her a shilling to go to the pictures.'

The record fell. 'Sherry, Sherry baby!'

The two blondes talked. 'One girl I know, she's only got to look at a boy and she's in trouble. She's fell twice.'

'She must need her eyesight tested.'

The boys came over, leaning elbows on the glass-topped pin-table. 'I was offered a job by a yid, four bob an hour digging up graves to get the rings off the corpses. "No thanks," I said. "I'd sooner get meself kept by some rich old bag!"' He blew smoke-rings at the blond girl. There was machine grease in his ear.

'I can't stand rich women—they muck you about. I was a delivery boy delivering vegetables. It got so much on me nerves I had to give it up, jacked it in. "Put them down here . . . no, here, I've changed me mind. I'm going to treat yer today." Then she'd hand me tuppence—she was Jewish. One day I lost me temper. "Eichmann shouldn't have bin executed, he should have bin made a knight," I said. She nearly hit the ceiling.'

'Coming outside?' said Dave. In the gathering dark boys kissed their girls, sitting astride their bikes, the girls leaning up against their thighs, coats open. The big bikes—the Triumph 500's, the BSA Gold Stars, the Bonnevilles—'I bet that can go!—were parked up the front right outside the door.

'There's a barn at the bottom of that hill—it's mostly fell down now—that's where we go with the girls. Off come the leather jackets—mine's got all wool inside, soft.' A Harley-Davidson swerved off into the night down the steep hill full of curves. The girl's hair blew black around her neck.

'I never sleep with no clothes on, I always make out I'm sleeping with a bird.' Slowly it got dark and the boys in their dirt-tight jeans turned on their headlamps, revving now and again as the summer night rolled down the North Circular Road. We walked round to the back of the café. The music blew out through the cracked windows: 'My heart cries for you, it even dies for you . . .'

'Lovely motors, these Yanks. A mate of mine had one, bought it for fifteen nicker and hammered the life out of it. One night the crank-shaft snapped and she slewed into a ditch. We reckoned she'd had it. She wasn't licensed nor insured nor nothing, so we got out and said good-bye.'

We strolled back to his bike. The sky was navy-blue. He put his hand down the back of my sweater.

'I love to hear the cats'-eyes go chunkety-chunk as the lorries hit 'em!'

'If I had a lot of money I'd take yer down to the South of France and give yer the time you deserved!'

'I thought of going back to screwing for a living, but then if I get three or five years cut out of me life . . . I can't do that . . . a great hunk out of me life . . . a great hunk.'

'I'd better take my watch off, it's not shockproof.' And then a little later: 'Pity we haven't got a Consul, see what I mean?'

'Why should we think ahead? What is there to think ahead to but growing old.'

A Norton with a blue tanker roared alongside us. Terry dragged his pointed toes along the ground.

'Fancy a burn-up, Dave?' They warmed the bikes up in the drive-in.

'Put yer arms tight around me and then relax. Okay?'

The wide road, lit by arc-lamps, stretched ahead. Over his shoulder I watched the speedometer quiver to ninety, then drop steeply as we approached a bend. He leant towards the kerb till my knee skimmed the road. The lights stopped, we pitched into darkness. He switched on his headlamp. Now the roar of the Norton screamed alongside us. Ahead was a crossroads. Neither bike slowed. The lights flicked to orange. Dave opened the throttle and zoomed across a lorry. We curved round the steel of its articulated side, the giant tyre spraying tiny pebbles into my face. The crash of metal against metal was drowned by engine roars, but I heard it and saw the riderless bike fling upright in the air behind us.

It was drizzling. The rain gathered in tiny clusters on his face. The lorry, unaware, had driven on. Dave took off his coat. 'Keep him warm, yer not dead till yer cold.' He bent over him and started to blow into his mouth. 'I learnt this in the Boy Scouts. Have you got a mirror on yer? I want to hold it to his mouth to see if he's breathing.' The back wheel of the smashed bike was still going round, making a faint ticking noise.

He stripped off his sweater and wrapped the boy's feet in it and then knelt beside him in his white T-shirt.

A lady motorist appeared. She got out of an Austin Princess. Little drops of water glistened on her black fur. 'Can I drive him to hospital?' In the sky the patterned moon shone through the split clouds.

'They won't let him in, he's dead.'

THE trial

'THEY MUST be from the striptease case!' Rube and I stood on the chequered stone floor of the London Sessions all got up in our white silk headscarves, waiting for Dave's case to be called.

'I remember when I was about ten years old, I was sittin' on the kitchen table havin' a wash when there's a terrific noise and in comes Bert, with three other fellas, rollin' a great safe! Me mum begins to holler and shout, "Get that thing out of here! I can't have that thing in here. You'll get me nicked." They pay no attention, they're trying all the different keys, and then Bert starts smashing at it with a jemmy and it flies open and out tumbles a load of papers and God knows what and bundles of notes. Then they carries it out the back door and buries it down the garden.

Now me mum's terrified that when they come to demolish the house they'll dig it up and have us all nicked!'

Dave's name echoed across the hall and Rube and I clattered up the wooden steps to the circle and sat in the front row, leaning on our hands.

'These knives found on your person could be very useful for opening window catches with, couldn't they?

'Could be very useful for eating yer dinner with as well.'

Dave stood aggressively in the box. He wore a black suit and a white lawn shirt with frills down the front.

'And what, may I ask, do you use these wire-clippers and crowbars for?' The smooth rolling tone of the barrister, sure beyond even cock.

'They're the tools of me trade, guv'ner. I'm a scrap merchant.'

'Well, what were they doing in your car?'

'I collect a lot of junk in me car. Perhaps if you had a car you'd collect junk in yours too.'

Nobody laughed except Rube in the gallery, opening wide her eyes and snorting into her pale pink jumper. 'It's that geyser's long grey hair-do making me piss meself.'

Later he was sent to stand in the dock and Rube and I hung over the edge to see him below, his hair thick and long around his ears. When all the evidence was given I was called as a character witness.

'Turn to the Judge and tell him when you first met Dave Macarthy. What did you discuss with him?'

'Morals. He decided finally after reading Marx and Lenin it would be better to get the things he wanted through changing the Government.' The Judge hid his smile in his hand.

We went across to the café for dinner while they decided the verdict. A couple of Dave's friends, arrogant and laughing, accompanied us. But Rube marched in front, pretending not to notice.

'Dave'll probably go to the Yorkshire same as us.'

'I wonder if old Macdonald's still there—the skinny screw in the cookhouse? Them great big ovens. The tricks we used to get up to . . .'

'I was on the farm—tractors—then I went out on a working party.'

'Wonder if Kelly's still there? Old Kelly always trying to cadge a feel . . .' A great hulk of a lorry drew up alongside the café, casting a vast black shadow over the table.

'Know what happened to him, Rube? Johnny jerked a finger at his mate. 'He's swinging in his cradle halfway up the building, whistling at some bird, and he lets the rope slip. Nearly chopped his hand off. Not only that, but he does the same thing the next morning whistling at the same bird.'

Rube tried not to laugh.

'Then me mate comes along in the night and nicked all the scaffold rings, so the next morning when I come to haul meself up in the cradle I'm only up fifty feet and the whole lot collapses!'

Rube gave a great shriek. At the same moment a jet of water poured from the ceiling hitting the lino and splashing up in a fine shower over the juke-box and tables.

'Lord have mercy, what's this?' A bucket was placed under the leak.

'Forgot to tell you he'd nicked them, did he?'

'Yeah, but at least the boss couldn't do me for that, seeing as I nearly broke me neck!'

Rube put on a record: 'In the night there are sights to be

seen, Stars like jewels on the crown of a queen...' I read the poster on the wall:

'Matsport Promotions Ltd. Wrestling, Popular Baths. Boxer versus Wrestler. The one and only Randolph Turpin versus Leon Arras. Quasimodo, the Hunchback Bellringer from Notre Dame, versus Dr Death, the Masked Mystery Man, Undefeated. Can he beat Quasimodo?'

'Here, Rube, you used to go out with Terry, didn't yer?' said Johnny.

Rube looked up.

'Well, the council sent his dad a bill for five pound' for the eight buckets of sand they used in clearing up the blood.'

Joe Brown sang on: "Then you were gone like a dream in the night. With you went my heart, my love and my light.'

We walked back to the court. They found Dave guilty. In the underground cells we went to say good-bye to him. Through the grating I could see a Milky Way paper, a blue plastic bottle and a Spangles packet. Dave kicked at the iron door and screamed, 'I'm bloody well going to get out of here.'

Rube and I cut down a side-street past a baby in a pram wrapped in a khaki blanket sucking at a teat stuck on a lemonade bottle, and headed for home. Towards us glided an apparition, a huge pink Cadillac pulling a pink caravan on which was written: MISS CAMAY IS HERE! WIN THIS CAR AND CARAVAN. ENTRY FORMS HERE. Music blared out of a loudspeaker. Inside the car sat a sulky blonde. The car drove dead slow and behind swarmed kids on roller skates or running, lollipops in mouths.

'Shame about that. Now you'll have to find yerself another bloke.'

'Yes.'

'That's the thing—what you don't get caught for you're entitled to do.'

PRISON visit

SNOW BLEW up in white sheets low across the black road and wind blew through the castle gates. We sat in rows on wooden benches, feet cold on the green lino. Rube and I sat close together talking in whispers.

'There'll be a crowd of them standing outside Jock's in the Arcade and a girl'll go by and one of them'll say, "I fancy that!" and another will say, "You won't get nothing out of her. She's no good." But if it's some slag what's bin with everyone he'll say, "Yeah, she's a good girl, you can get the lot out of her." '

An old girl with a henna rinse chatted to her daughter: 'She liked the fur—got it up Brixton Market—it was a good fur, nice colour and all, but it turned out too short after she'd 'ad her operation up the hospital; she's taller than ever.'

'Oh, he was awfully sociable—he talked to everyone, even the women.'

'Here,' said Rube, 'a man in my work asked me out today. Brian would be wild if he found out. This fella asked me to go for a drink and then go back to his house—said his mum would be out. He's a handsome fella, short with wavy black hair—he works in front of me and he stares at me all day.'

'The trouble with Dave is he's too bloody vain. He used to twist me arm and say, "Who's the best-looking boy in the road?" and I'd say Fred Hewar and he'd twist it further till I shrieked and I had to say David Macarthy, then he'd let me go . . .'

The names were read out briefly and the visitors filed across the prison yard strung out, the young woman carrying her baby, followed by two little girls in fur coats and white bonnets trotting over the icy concrete yard and into the Nissen hut.

'They look good, them stockings—seams are very provocative,' said Rube.

Dave come in, his hair cut short, wearing a blue serge battledress. 'I'm writing a book. It's going to be called *In Out In.*'

We sit on tin chairs around a tin table and two prisoners serve cups of grey tea and little threepenny packets of biscuits.

'So what's going on with you?' Dave smokes aggressively.

'Oh, yeah—we went to help with the spring cleaning in Michael Wilding's flat. You should have seen the place. The bath was all pink and sunken. Directly I saw it I had to have a bath. Off come me clothes and there I am lounging back like Elizabeth Taylor, ton of perfume rising up with the steam. The bed had a satin coverlet and lemon blankets with

satin binding, and a bamboo bar with every sort of drink, the walls covered with thick green paper and green satin curtains . . . Ooh, mate.'

At the next table a sleek young man was entertaining his friend. 'Have you got all you want, Alfred?'

'See this skirt?' The fat woman at the next table bunched

her brown skirt between her hands. 'A month ago this skirt was too tight for me and look at it now—I can get whole handfuls of it. That's dieting, that is.'

'I had to evict me father-in-law. He was sixty-five and his wife died and he began bringin' in old women and misbehavin' with them in his room. We had a terrible law-case, me standing in one box yelling me head off and him in another yelling back. The names he called me . . .'

Two warders walked around the room past the black notices saying what we mustn't do.

'Give us a quid, Rube.'

'Here, you'll get me nicked.'

'You can stick it under the table with yer chewing gum and then fetch another cup of tea, and I'll take it.'

Rube went to get the tea. Dave stretched out his hands on the table. 'They say Borstal's all right—sort of university for them what can't afford Oxford.'

He touched my cheek with his finger. 'Is it too late to get meself a decent education?'

A warder leant against the wall, above his head a notice: VISITORS PASSING ANYTHING TO PRISONERS WILL BE PROSECUTED.

'A bloke in the next cell done himself in—stood on a chair in a pot of piss and plugged himself into the light socket. He got a Dear John—a letter from his bird saying she didn't want to know any more.'

Rube came back with the tea. It spilt over the edge of the white mug and made a little pool on the tin table. Dave dipped his fingertip in and drew a ship. Outside the snow fluttered past, clean in the dirty air, and then fell grey in the concrete yard. A bell went and visitors got up to go. For a moment men clung to their wives. A girl ground painted lips against her boy's teeth and a tongue stretched out for a last feel.

And then it was all quiet. No one said good-bye, but the men lined up through the door and straggled out of the hut, and the visitors straggled towards the giant gate and stopped in a bunch.

'Hey,' said Rube, 'look at them blacks.'

Just inside the gates two Coloured men were arguing excitedly with the warders. 'Have you ever seen anything like the state of their tarts?'

Suddenly the two warders catch hold of one of the women and drag her down the passage—the other is hauled by the arm. Someone unlocks the huge door and first one and then the other is flung out into the road. Their men hurry after them. The Irish blonde staggers to her feet, her eye cut, both her hands bleeding and her stockings torn, opens her mouth and pours forth abuse. The Coloureds talk fast in unintelligible language. The other woman with frizzed red-rinsed hair and a scar across her forehead shouts. 'Dirty, bleeding cowards—you didn't dare touch our men.' She is about forty and wears a low-cut dress, no stockings and high suede shoes. Her feet bulge over; her legs are mottled.

Muttering threats, the oddly assorted foursome hobble down the road.

'Cor,' says Rube. 'I couldn't fancy that roasted!'

DEATH of an old scrubber

SYLVIE AND I stood outside the rag-shop, leaning against a notice—HIGHEST PRICES PAID FOR OLD GOLD AND SILVER AND ARTIFICIAL TEETH—and waited for the totters. Gusts of wind and rain hurtled over the debris and the women turned up their collars.

Mrs Hardy hurried across the road, her one black tooth sticking out between her lips, clasping her tattered coat around her.

'Hello, my ducks,' she said. Her old canvas shoes were full of holes.

'You'll get wet,' I said.

'It don't matter, it'll clean me coat. Know what? I'm courting again.'

'You're not.'

'Yes, I am. I met him up the Mission at one of them

shilling dinners for Old Age Pensioners. He kept asking me
to go to tea, but I didn't like to go, because I knew he had
a place on his own and his wife's bin dead eighteen months—
you know what men are.'

'All right—if you keep yer hand on yer halfpenny,' said
Sylvie.

'Well, I went up to see him Sunday. Cooked his dinner for
him. It was ever so cold up there. "You ought to have got a
fire going for me," I says. "You cold, duck?" he says. "Get
under them covers." '

The women laugh. 'Never know when they're past it,
do they?'

' "Blimey," I says when he asked me to go and be his
housekeeper. "Don't swear in 'ere," he says. "This is God's
house." "Well," I says, "God might tempt me. You've got
an apple tree down your garden, haven't you?" "Yes," he
says. "Well, Adam tempted Eve with an apple." I don't want
to get married again. I had a rotten husband, he gave me
thirty-eight bob a week and stopped two bob income tax.
This one's seventy-four, but he's got fifty quid and 'e wants
to take me away to Bromsgrove for a fortnight. I've bin a
widow fourteen years, so I know how to look after meself.
Anyway, if I don't there's not much chance of me getting in
the family way.'

A totter loomed into sight through the drizzle, pushing his
barrow piled with old clothes, gas-fires, bits of linoleum and
second-hand shoes, past the half-demolished slums. Old Loo
and Kit and May crowded round him, rapidly picking and
discarding.

'Any piece threepence. Nice pair of woollen undies here.'

He held up an off-white rag. 'Let's 'ave it,' said Mrs Hardy. She took it and quickly scrutinised it. 'It's rotten at the crutch.' She chucked it back at him.

'See Scummy Lil yesterday? She come here and was after buying a pair of drawers. Held 'em up against her, she did. "Come off it," I says. "you don't need no drawers in your job." '

Another barrow came round the corner through the drizzle and the women hurried towards it. Mrs Hardy coughed violently and when the fit was over sprayed her throat with a black syringe. 'See what the doctor give me? Good, ain't it?' She unscrewed her ear-rings. 'Here, love, you wear these. Go on. Yer a long time dead, girl! Get out and enjoy yerself.'

The next afternoon the women huddled in the rag-shop waiting for the totters. It was snowing outside. 'Yeah, it was about nine last night. I saw the ambulance outside her house. I went out and I met the ambulance man just coming out of the telephone kiosk. "Is it old Mrs Hardy?" I says. "Yeah," he says, "she's beyond all 'uman aid." "Oh, my Gawd," I says.

'She was a scrubber all her life. Ever since she was fourteen worked in that bagwash—boiling hot in summer, damp and draughty in the winter. Surprised it didn't finish her off sooner.'

'Anyways she was paid up with her insurance. It's better to pay yer shilling a week and know you're going to be properly buried—not in with some stranger.'

'I'd sooner have an 'orse and cart. You get to yer grave too quick in a motor.'

'I had this lodger died in bed. I had coal-black hair and I

wore a pink satin blouse. I laid him out and tied his jaw up with a hankie to the bedrail. When my husband come in he says, "What you done that for? They'll think you strangled him." '

Two spades walked by, hands dug in pockets, shoulders hunched, the snow white on their black curls. 'See them, they live off Kit-E-Kat. The woman in the cut-price store told me one come in there last week and bought a dozen tins. "My Gawd," she says, "however many cats you got?" "I ain't got no cats, lady," he says, "I've got six kids." '

Sylvie and I sat down on a vast bale of rags and played cards.

'Are you frightened of dying, Sylvie?'

'No, you can't get hurt when yer dead.'

Fat Loo, her frizzy hair sticking out stiffly, sorted idly through a pile of rags. 'I says to Arthur, "If I ever die bury me with me knickers on." And 'e says, "Whoever do you think's going to take liberties with you?" "You never know," I says. I told old Carny the undertaker, "I want a pair of thick woollen drawers on to save me getting a cold in me crumpet. Anything but red. Red's danger." "I'll make a nice box of cold meat of you," he says.'

'Ever seen one of them urns?' says Fat Loo. 'Well, you wouldn't think I could fit in one of them, would yer now?'

'I wouldn't like to be cremated—you can't have no visitors to your grave. Just shut up in that little urn—it ain't much fun.'

'But I reckon it stops the spread of diseases—the bodies don't get handled so much. The soil must throw up something bad.'

'They reckon you're in a standing position when you're cremated. When they open the drapes you work along on a slide till you're in an upright position and then the relatives say good-bye.'

'Hear about Mr Marple over the road? He won seventy quid on the pools and 'e's spent it all on a stone for 'is grave. He's got it propped up in his back yard waitin'!'

'I'm going home. Coming?' said Sylvie.

We took a short cut over the debris. Some boys had lit a fire by a pile of old rubble. They sat round it on abandoned armchairs with bellies gouging horsehair and bugs, cooking chestnuts.

'Remember the night Terry got killed? I was over your house washing me hair and Rube came screaming down the road, "His eyes come out, his teeth went through the back of his head and the handlebars went through his chest." Poor Rube, she was getting engaged in a fortnight.'

It had stopped snowing now. The slush oozed over the pavement into the clogged gutter. Black smoke billowed across the yellow sky. The factory siren hooted five o'clock. We went by the laundry to collect our wash. On the door was pinned a note: 'Owing to the passing of Mrs Hardy the bagwash won't be ready till Wednesday.'

THE tally man

WE HURRIED down the Old Kent Road on our way to the Union at ten o'clock on a Friday night. We'd been in the Kings Arms all evening but hadn't seen anything we fancied.

'Ever bin in one of them bed and breakfast places?' Jeanie points at a cardboard sign stuck in a window.

'Yeah, but I had to run out before the breakfast,' says Sylvie.

'Remember that Fred? One night he says to me, "Come on, we're going to a club," and he only takes me to a knocking shop . . . Cor!' says Jean.

Sylvie pisses in the road. 'Quick Sylv, there's a car comin' in ter park!' The headlamps beam. 'Pull yer drawers up!'

'It's all right.' She jumps to her feet. 'I don't wear no drawers Friday nights—it's 'andy . . .'

We press into the packed pub, deafened by the scream of love through the mike. 'Nothing can keep him from me.' Then the singer turns his back to the audience and whispers the next line—then suddenly he swings round to face them, yelling out the final chorus 'He *is* my destiny,' his plump face sweating. Two fifteen-year-olds twist by the toilets.

Three blokes, the hard type, are chatting us up. They wear dark suits. 'Here, I'll have the thick-set one,' whispers Sylvie.

'Oh you lovely little thing—you look the naïve type,' he says to Sylvie with her dozen times bleached hair piled on top of her head and her scruff of fur pinned to her red suit. 'Mind me mink marmot!'

'Cor I fancy your mate!'

'What in this weather?'

'Comin' over Bertie's club?'

So we pile onto hot knees in the Zephyr and burn through Brixton.

'Oh I knew I was missin' somethin',' says Sylvie, 'me ear-rings, me gold ear-rings . . . shoot round the market and I'll buy another pair for one and a tanner . . .'

The girls sway in the Zephyr and sing:

'I like 'em. I like 'em when they're fair, fat and forty . . .'

'Here, Jeanie, remember when I went ten stone?'

A sleezy thrower-out lets us in up a red-carpeted staircase into a plushy room with white plastic seats around the walls, wine wallpaper and a walnut bar, smoky and thick with young old men in slick suits and clean shirts. Dick buys a round of Scotch . . . gin and lime for the girls. Another man joins us. 'Heard the news? They've planted the Bus Murder on me brother . . . put a fuckin' key in his pocket and all.'

Bob buys a second round, taking a big bundle of notes from his pocket. 'Hear what happened to Jess? He robbed this bank and he was gettin' away with the money over this dirty great wall when he slips and chops the top of his finger off on the glass. So he's there on the ground lookin' for it. He can't go without it because they could get a fingerprint off of it and do him for the bank robbery.'

'What line of business are you in?'

'Motor cars—I've bin away on me holidays in Lincoln three years, I only came out last Monday week.' He smiles a quick smile on his little rat face. 'Got a good motor down the sales—Jaguar Mark 7, 1953—a hundred nicker, going to spray it—should get three-fifty for it.'

The man whose brother's been planted for the Bus Murder buys another round of doubles—'I can't drink any more'— but he buys them just the same, paying with a bundle of pound notes which he keeps in a special pocket in the inside thigh flap of his jacket. 'Life's treating me pretty fair—the old pocket's bulging.'

'Pour them on the carpet beside you,' says Jeanie. 'Nobody will take notice.'

A queer gets up on the mike, places one hand on his hip and sings:

> *I wanta boy, I wanta boy*
> *I wanta nice young man*
> *Who will understand,*
> *Get up them stairs and that's not all . . .*

Signet rings flash. Gold watches with gold expandable

straps, light leather shoes and loud laughter. The queer waggles his arse and sings:

> *I wanta boy I wanta boy*
> *Not as a toy*
> *But to enjoy*
> *I wanta great big beautiful boy!*

Up in Bertie's under the twisting railway arches of Brixton we sit, the six of us around a low table on shiny couches—the boys with their flicked-back hair and we with knees pressed tight together, suspenders bumping under thigh-tight skirts.

'You all right fer undersets?'

He was a big bloke in his thirties, blond hair and skin-tight trousers.

'I'm a Tally Man, the name's Barny. Carpets, briefs, cookin' utensils, you name it I've got it.'

Jeanie's 'kitten-kut' orange hair and bony legs stiff in the high white shoes. She leans across to me and whispers, 'He's all right, he's got a ton of money . . .'

Dick explained the motor car business to Jeanie. 'You can start with a lot of old bangers and make twenty or thirty quid on each one. This Old Kent Road is a perfect site—you get a lot of rough diamonds round here who'll buy up these cars. You make much more than someone with a bloody great showroom and a load of overheads. People are frightened to go in and posh people make sure they're getting their money's worth. Ten per cent of our cars get snatched back and another thirty per cent we have to give a little longer over payments. Our job is to smooth away the mountains so people can see their way to buying a car. It doesn't matter to us if they don't complete payments . . . it's the finance company what takes the rap. If they lose too much money they won't finance you any more so you go to another company. When no finance company will take you on you go bust, and go into some other business.'

Barny leans towards me. 'I've bin with all sorts of girls but it's the decent girls like you that I prefer. If you keep on comin' down here you won't stay decent.'

Sylvie gets up and dances with Dick. Her eyes peep over his padded shoulder.

'I've bin with some floosies in me time but I've never mentioned me wife's name to them—I wouldn't do it, I think too much of her,' says Barny.

'It's the girls that play hard to get that I like the best.

'I was a truck driver eleven years—leave for Scotland twelve o'clock at night—eleven fuckin' years. We used to have a great time—Liverpool, Hull, Manchester, Newcastle—I know them all. Manchester's the best of the lot—the clubs there— you couldn't get better clubs anywhere . . . If you had the price of a drink or a lodging for the night you'd always have the drink and fuck the lodging—sleep in the cab.

'The country'd go broke if the labour government got in . . . they haven't any money—you've gotta have money to do anything . . .

'I'd love to make you into a really bad girl . . . It's not the same now since the Transport started banging down all their regulations. You don't get the same crowd on the roads . . . lousy the drivers now and the boys tell me the clubs in Manchester aren't the same any more . . .

'But it's a good life for a Tally Man—I'm usin' me brains

to the best of me ability—what the government calls Free Enterprise—

'Me mates are all fiddlers . . .'

Sylvie bounced through the door and sat down next to me. 'He asks me to come for a little walk underneath the arches —told me he was happily married and all that game and he didn't believe in knockin' it off with other birds and ten minutes later he's saying, "The trouble with me is I'm over-sexed . . ." '

Barny buys another round of drinks. 'There ain't no consummation in philosophy and I like consummation . . . will you let me see you home?'

Now the flowers arrive. Women in cheap coats and slippers come to the door with bunches of roses. Then a cross of lilies and fern—'For Mrs Hardy with our condolences from all in Speke Road.' A little boy with a bouquet of yellow flowers trots down the street in plimsolls, his dog runs at his heels.

The Rolls Royce hearse arrives followed by another Rolls. Seven women stand watching on the pavement, hands stuck in their aprons, talking among themselves.

Mr Carny and the men get out of the hearse and disappear inside the house. They carry out the bunches of flowers and pile them on top. Last of all they carry out Mrs Hardy . . . and her daughter and granddaughter and son-in-law and the brother-who-hasn't-died climb into the mourners' car.

And off they drive up the hill—Mrs Hardy in a black Rolls Royce: 'I told him I wanted to be buried just up the road . . . not too far from home. I was born in Battersea—I've lived all me life in Battersea—I don't want to go and get buried in Wandsworth, do I?'

I go up the road to meet Barny—twelve o'clock on the corner.

He still wears the same shiny suit in the sunlight. There are black scoops under his small eyes. 'Jump in!'

Into the new Austin van with the grating over the windows; in the back are the goods—sheets and skirts and petticoats in cellophane and black and yellow boxes.

'You get a foot in the door, start off with a few soft goods . . . a couple of shirts for Dad—shoes for Johnny, an underset for Mum—soon they're buying everything off of you—bedroom suites, curtains, kitchen sets, cardigans . . . Once you've got yer foot in the door you keep it there . . . you hold on to 'em and you never let 'em go . . .'

He drove hard through Wandsworth, swinging round the corner past the tall flats, like a man who is on the road all day, and up over a cascade of railway lines flowing towards the Junction.

'For some old dears it's the advent of the week—they don't have no other social calls—they get the teapot all set out . . .

'My wife's all right but all she knows is the home and the kids . . .'

In Brixton he swung down a street, rows of dreary little two-storey houses with box windows sticking out towards the broken pavement . . .

'Sixty per cent of me calls are black—I'm like the white hunter, at the end of the street you can practically hear the Tom Tom going "Sandy's back again." '

He stops the car and takes the black book. He bangs loudly on the door. The street is still. A kid plays on the pavement with a Saxa salt box and a handful of pebbles. His red sweater is safety-pinned together. Barny bangs on the door again, louder this time. Someone peers through the curtains next door. Opposite a woman comes out to shake her mat. At last she comes.

'Can you leave it fer this week I'm a bit short?'

'Come on, you're eight pound' owing. You'd better let me have ten bob.'

'Me husband didn't let me have much this week.' A woman goes by with a baby-laden push-chair.

'Well, it's Tuesday, ain't it? Tuesday Family Allowance day—who keeps the kid's books you or 'im?'

A tiny tot peers round her legs. 'All right then, wait a minute . . .'

A young man walks past; his sleeves rolled up his brown arms, his jeans faded and white with brick-dust—he whistles as he goes.

Barny gets back into the van.

'Two pair of good blankets she's owing for.'

'Why don't you take them back?'

'Take 'em back? I wouldn't put those blankets back in here—the van would crawl away. Anyway she's a pawn-shop call. You sell 'em a pair of blankets and ten minutes later she's sold 'em fer cash to a woman down the road and she's got to keep on paying me five bob a week for something she hasn't even got. You don't know how daft some of 'em are— they think they're being clever—have four or five Tally Men and something different off of each.

' "Which are you?" they say when you come to the door. They never know what they're paying for or when the payments are done—you can go on collecting ten bob a week for a year.

Yet his blue suit was shoddy—his flash tie pin was only brass. 'And the further they get in debt the dirtier they become—more like animals they live some of 'em—when they open the front door you can smell the filth. I have to smoke like mad while I'm writin' in me book.'

There is a smell of coal being emptied down a chute.

'I'm sick of the Coloureds—I want some nice young house-wifes to cheer me up on a Tuesday.' He skews his broad shoulders round towards me with a whiff of after-shave and short blond hair . . . 'There's this nurse—I call on her ten o'clock on a Saturday morning and she's on night duty, you see—so when she opens the door—"Oh," she says, "excuse me, I was just havin' a bath" and I goes in and she makes me a cup of tea and I can tell she ain't got nothin' on under her dressing-gown—each time she moves she lets me see a bit more and a bit more—But then I can't be sure . . . you can always make mistakes, can't yer?'

He looks in his book. 'Only a couple more calls and then we can go and have some beer. Most of 'em you can make 'em buy anything. Twenty-five per cent don't know what they're paying for and fifty per cent don't want the stuff anyway.'

We drive up a hill past a telephone box with shattered windows. The tiny pieces of glass glint on the pavement. On a wall is painted KEEP THE BLACKS OUT FOR A WHITE CHRISTMAS.

'H.O. Husband objects . . . they're the best of all because they'll do anything to stop their husbands finding out. After a bit you loan 'em ten pound' at the rate of seven shillings in the pound to be paid back in ten weeks—So there you are, collectin' twenty-seven bob a week. Then if after five weeks they're a bit short you say, "All right, love. I'll help you out, I'll tell yer what I'll do. I'll lend yer another tenner." So you give 'em another ten, subtract what they still owe yer from the first ten—say it's five with another thirty-five bob on top fer the interest and then they usually give yer five bob— "You've bin good to me"—and all that. Then you walk out of the flat leavin' three pound' and they've got to pay you twenty-seven bob fer the next ten weeks—oh it never ends . . .'

We tread softly over the carpeted saloon. 'Have a gin and lime.

'There are a million and one ways of getting money. You hold the threat of court over them. But that's your last resort. Once you've used that yer finished because you've lost the one bar in yer hand . . .

'I reckon my wife gets a good bargain—granted I'm not at home much—the trouble with me is I can't sit still—and anyway I've got to be out and about the clubs at night, that's where you make your contacts. But my wife gets the extra clothes. I get plenty of perks as a Tally Man. I can get a twenty-six-guinea suit for thirteen guineas.'

'Like the one you've got on?'

'I'd hate to do anything to offend you but you've got the finest pair of legs I've seen in a long time . . . I've got an idea you don't really like havin' anything to do with men.'

'I like talking.'

'Well, you'll be safe with me. I'm not a pursuer. I've got a mate and a girl in the street's only gotta smile at him and he's got her phone number—but I just grabs what comes along.'

Back in the van he says, 'I've gotta call on a nigger tomorrow. His wife's a great big Zulu. I think he's trying to pull me. He's got a big scar down one side of his face—and he'll have a scar down the other if he's not careful.

'They mustn't be too price-conscious because our stuff's pretty dear—it has to be, after all they get it delivered to the door.'

We drive past torn buildings and mud swamps scattered with floating newspapers. 'Palaces, ain't they?' he says. 'You've gotta be hard in our business. If anyone conned me, I'd go after 'im and if I didn't get 'im the first night I'd get 'im the next . . .' He sticks out his lower lip, curling it over the top one like James Cagney playing a Chicago gangster.

'But I'm a playboy at heart—and you've gotta live, haven't yer? To live the way I like to live it costs. The man that spends his leisure digging the garden's an idiot . . . Yeah, well perhaps he is happy—they say all idiots are happy . . .'

We swung over a railway bridge. Dense smoke spewed out through the railings and stopped by some council flats. 'Who gives anything away? No one. Everybody takes. No one ever gives yer anything. I'm not a cynic. I'd hate yer to think I were.'

The little creases squeeze round his narrow blue eyes. 'I'd love to give you a good time—I could give you such a time as you'd never forget.'

He climbs out of the van putting a suit over his arm. 'Come on, I'm selling a suit to a darkie.'

He banged on the door and a gentle-faced Negro let us in. 'Hello, sah.'

'I've brought the suit—it's a good one.'

He held up the cheap grey serge and shook it out. 'Only needs a rub with an iron, try it on.'

He lived in one bow-faced room and I looked the other way while he tried it. In one corner was a neat cot and a sleeping baby, black face snudged against the white sheet. The cooker was under the window next to a shiny walnut radiogram and beyond a double bed. On the other wall was the dressing-table with a small mirror above it in which the Negro bent up to see himself in his new suit.

'Good, ain't it?' says Barny, holding down the back of the jacket.

'I think it's a little tight mister—see, I can't button it up . . .'

The front of the double-breasted suit didn't meet by about four inches. 'Oh no, you never do 'em up these days,' says Barny, 'it's the fashion to leave 'em hanging open . . . I wouldn't be seen dead with me jacket buttoned.'

'All right, I'll have it, mister.' Barny lets go of the back of the jacket. 'It's twelve pound'—you can give me two now and pay it off a pound a week how's that?'

The baby woke and started to whimper so he picked her up in his great arms and put a record on the gramophone. 'She likes music,' he says smiling.

Outside Barny bent himself in half. 'They just make me roll up . . .'

We drove back towards home. 'You see the blacks have only got half the brain cells to what we've got. They never had a civilisation, they never even invented the wheel—what jerks to go through life without inventing the wheel.'

Evening and the girls wear cotton dresses showing teenage knees and loll against the off-licences eating fish and chips as we go by. The dogs snuff the de-housed rats in the latest demolished terraces. He drops me off. On the corner a group of jean-boys are gathered round bicycles and scooters, hoisting Coca-Cola bottles to their lips, and all the chimneys of Battersea are reaching to the sky and puffing mauve clouds into the cloudless summer evening.

THE children

THE TEACHERS are out on strike and troops of children trudge the streets with sticks.

'I've had me 'air curled today.'

The toddlers squat on the pavement with bits of chalk and draw.

'Me mum got a new baby on the HP.'

Over the mud and rubble, they go to where the crane smashes down the slum clearance houses; red legs and brown coats and the rattle of trains swinging along the line.

'Our teacher says, "God made everything." "What are the factories for then, miss?" I says.'

Through the white-tiled alley with its millions of messages scrawled in pencil and lipstick—RUSSIA IS BEST—to where the new flats tower above them and onto the playground.

'Know what my Bill done yesterday? He says to me,

"Here, my Doreen, get on yer bike and pedal down to Wandsworth Bridge and chuck these in the river," and he give me two plastic sandwich-bags full of pearl necklaces and rings. So I cycles up onto Wandsworth Bridge and when I chucks them over the side all the bags is full of air so it doesn't sink, and then it starts to sink and all the bubbles come up and I'm scared someone going to see me . . .'

Harry slides down the slide on his back, eyes closed. At the bottom he lies luxuriously, legs drawn up; the ingrained dirt makes black lines in the open cracks across his knee-caps. Harry lies while other children pile up behind, his face wiped clean by the scullery flannel, his hands clasped over his stomach. 'Shut-up,' he says. 'I'm thinkin'.'

On they go past the torn buildings and mud swamps, scattered with bricks and floating newspapers. 'I reckon the Queen's a show-off,' says Harry. Down through the tangle of grass on the churchyard graves to the beach and to the mud stretching out to the water.

'You know what newly-weds do? Have a bit of a kiss and a cuddle. I know the facts of life, I do. What would they want to watch telly for?'

Johnny throws a stick at a swan.

'Me mum don't care what time I come in of a night. She's always watching telly.'

'Well, yer mum ain't a newly-wed, is she?'

The barges glide past with small men riding on their backs. Trains rattle over the bridge from Fulham.

'We was playin' mothers and fathers in the deckhouse of that old barge, me and Moraine in one bed and Bobby was our baby in the other. Then I done it to Moraine.'

'Did you let him take yer drawers down?'

'No, of course I didn't. I took them down meself,' says ten-year-old Moraine, indignant.

Great gusts of black smoke blow sideways out of the four chimneys of Fulham gasworks across a streaky sky.

'Did yer like it?'

'No, not much.'

'You can be sent to prison for doing that. A girl down our street was sent to prison for havin' a baby.'

Suddenly the sky splits and the black rain bounces off the river. The children scramble up the wall and run for shelter past a tin suitcase and an old piano, around a crooked tree.

'Come on, 'Arry. Mum'll kill yer if yer get wet'—Moraine catches five-year-old Harry by the hand and runs, skinny legs in her velvet dress, skipping over the puddles.

Printed in the United States
by Baker & Taylor Publisher Services